The Shy Guy's Guide to Dating

Also by Barry Dutter

Everything I Really Need to Know I Learned from Television

How to Be a Hollywood Superstar

The SHY GUY'S Guide to Dating

Barry Dutter

ST. MARTIN'S PRESS
New York

THOMAS DUNNE BOOKS.
An imprint of St. Martin's Press.

Design by Kathryn Parise

Library of Congress Cataloging-in-Publication Data

Dutter, Barry.
The shy guy's guide to dating / by Barry Dutter.
p. cm.
ISBN 0-312-18757-2
1. Men—United States—Psychology. 2. Dating (Social customs)—United States. 3. Bashfulness—United States. I. Title.
HQ1090.3.D87
646.7'7'081—dc21 98-5090
CIP

10 9 8 7 6 5 4 3 2

Dedications

I'd like to dedicate this book to my old pal Tommy Diaz, who first introduced me to the phrase "Shy Guy." I once asked Tommy what approach he used to meet girls. He responded, "I dunno—I guess I use the Shy Guy approach."

I'd also like to dedicate it to all the girls who ever rejected me, without whom this book could not have been written.

I'd like to thank my Shy Guy buddies, whose wacky misadventures provided much free material for this book: Ray Podolla, Dave Polito, Dave McCormick, Kerwin McLachlan, "Jazzy" Johnny Salerno, and Warren Mateychak.

I'd also like to dedicate this book to my sister's boyfriend, Kevin Levi, who I forgot to mention in the introduction to my last book.

Most of all, I'd like to thank my old buddy Charlie Bihler, who made so many valuable contributions to this book, I almost feel I should give him some money. I said "almost." He'll have to settle for a dedication!

Thanks for all the input, Charlie. The book is better for you having been included. Good luck with your new marriage. Ellen is a great gal, and I wish you the best.

I'd like to thank someone who was always there for me, who never let me down, who showed me the facts of life (and not just the kind with Tootie and Mrs. Garrett), who inspired me, who made me laugh, made me cry and lifted me up where I belonged. Of course, I'm speaking about my television. Thanks, TV—I couldn't have done it without you.

Oh, yes—a very special shout out should also go out to *Charlie's Angels,* without whom I might not have made it through puberty!

I'd like to thank my original editor, Jason Rekulak, who first saw the potential in *The Shy Guy's Guide to Dating* and offered some fine suggestions, and my final editor, Hannah Thomson, whose contributions greatly improved the book. Hannah, thank you for your patience. You are an excellent editor. I'd also like to give major snaps to the intern at St. Martin's who originally found my proposal in the slush pile and thought, "Hey, this guy might be on to something here!"

I'd also like to thank the nice people who published my first two books, *Everything I Really Need to Know I Learned from Television* (Applause Books, $7.95), and *How to Be a Hollywood Superstar* (General Publishing Group, $7.95). By a strange coincidence, both of these books are still available from their respective publishers.

Contents

Ya know, a lot of people think shyness is a disease.
But I think it's okay.

—SYLVESTER STALLONE IN *ROCKY* (1976)

Introduction

Okay, so you're shy. You're not comfortable meeting girls. You have problems getting dates. When you talk to a girl you're attracted to, you freeze up, get nervous, and tongue-tied. Well, guess what—you're not alone.

There are lots of guys out there just like you—guys who seem cursed to go through life without a partner. By this point, you've probably convinced yourself that you're never going to meet anyone, that you're going to spend the rest of your days hanging out with the guys, shooting pool on Saturday nights.

Well it doesn't have to be that way. And I should know, because I've been in your shoes.

When I was younger, I had a severe shyness complex. I was so shy, I couldn't look anyone in the eye when I spoke to them. I used to keep my head hung low. Very low. People used to have to look at the top of my head as they spoke to me. I hated meeting new people—absolutely hated it.

As you might imagine, a shyness complex like this completely prevented me from meeting any girls. I never had a date in high school. I never went to the prom, or to any of the school dances. Sure, I wanted to go out with girls, but there was only one problem—I was too shy to do anything about it.

I used to have fantasies about how I could trick girls into going out with me, without my having to actually go through the trauma of asking them on dates. Of course, I never acted on any of these fantasies. But I still had hope—after all, Hollywood had taught me that if you wait around long enough, eventually the girl of your dreams will ask you out. Well, that never happened to me—at least not with any girl I had any interest in dating.

I remember a friend once tried to convince me to ask out a girl. I argued against the idea, saying it wasn't safe. I told my friend, "The only safe relationships are the ones in your mind." Pretty sad, but it's true, in a twisted kind of way. In your dreams, you can have any girl you want, with no repercussions whatsoever. But in the real world, there are no guarantees. Why give up a healthy fantasy life for the ugly reality of potential rejection?

Although I fantasized about the opposite sex constantly, my actual social life was nonexistent. I must say, though, I had an incredible sex life in my dreams. I had a totally serious plan all worked out to steal Cindy Crawford away from Richard Gere. (I mean, come on—how hard would that have been? It's not like Richard Gere was going to put up any kind of a fight!)

Eventually, I abandoned my fantasy world for the real one, with all the pleasure and pain and surprises and fear and heartache that it offers. In the real world, you don't always have control over what happens, and therein lies the risk.

But if you ever intend to have a full and satisfying life, you've got to take chances. You've got to actually talk to that cute girl in the back row of your science class, regardless of how difficult it may be for you. Because no matter how many friends you have, no matter how much satisfaction you get from your job, and how much love and support you get from your family, without a girl by your side, there's always going to be a big hole in your life.

Sure, you can try and convince yourself otherwise. You can argue, "But I've got a very fulfilling job! And I have a great time when I go out with my friends!" But at the end of the day, when you lie alone in bed, you'll know the truth—that there is something missing.

We all have a deep, ingrained desire to share our lives with someone. This is the most basic and primal human need. Sure, you can have a decent life alone, but it will be infinitely richer if you have someone there beside you. When you're younger, you can go out with your friends and have a great time. But as you get older, it's just not the same. Those same experiences would be more enjoyable, more meaningful, with the girl you love alongside you.

Being in a serious relationship certainly makes Valentine's Day a hell of a lot easier to deal with. And there is something to be said for steady sex, too! Anyone who's in a serious relationship could tell you that. That's just one of the many fringe benefits!

I remember being at the Jersey shore, at the age of sixteen, seeing a pretty girl in the water, walking up to her, standing next to her, desperate to talk to her. All I had to do was ask her "How's the water?" That's all. Three little words. But I couldn't do it. I was too shy. And so I walked away, leaving behind an ocean full of missed opportunities.

When I was seventeen, I again approached pretty girls at the Jersey shore, and this time, I was so horny that I was actually able to strike up conversations with them. But I was unable to actually ask the girls out on dates. At the conclusion of a conversation, I would say, "It was nice meeting you," and walk away, leaving the girl to wonder why I hadn't had the guts to ask the question I had obviously been leading up to the entire time. It tore me up inside, not being able to ask out those girls—to carry the ball all the way down the field and then fumble on the one yard line—but there was nothing I could do about it.

I was shy.

I finally asked a girl out at the age of eighteen, in my first year of college. I went on my first date at nineteen, and I was in my early twenties when I had sex with a real live woman for the first time.

I wasted a lot of years wallowing in shyness, and I hate to see anyone making the same mistakes I made. My main problem, when it came to girls, was that I never had any encouragement. If only I had had a mentor—someone to coach me, to guide me, to tell me all the right words to say, the right moves to make, and when to make them.

My parents divorced when I was nine, so my dad wasn't around that much. (To Dad's credit, he once tried to offer me a helpful dating tip. He advised, "You should learn how to dance! Girls like guys who can dance!" He told me that when I was twenty-five. Good ol' Dad—he was a fine role model in many ways, but giving pointers on dating was not his specialty!)

My older brother mostly hung out with his own friends and did his own thing. I never forgot the one piece of dating advice he did give me. My brother said the best time to approach girls is when you are on vacation. Odds are, you will never see any of these girls again, so it doesn't matter if they reject you. One of the biggest fears holding back a Shy Guy is the thought of having to face a girl again after she has rejected him. By only approaching girls while you are on vacation, you eliminate the risk.

I never forgot my brother's advice, and I've put it into use on all my subsequent vacations. My only wish was that he had told me that at the beginning of the summer, so I wouldn't have wasted another season. That one piece of encouragement meant so much to me.

As I've grown older, I've done my best to encourage my friends in all their romantic pursuits. Usually I wind up going overboard and giving my friends too much encouragement, but you can see where it's coming from. A little bit of encouragement can make the difference between your friend meeting his future wife or walking away at the end of the night saying, "I really wish I had said something!" To this day, it still rankles me to see any guy walk away from an opportunity to meet a cute girl because he let his shyness get in the way.

One of my proudest moments as a supportive friend came one night when my buddy Ted was in a bar, chatting up a young lady he was extremely attracted to. They hit it off and talked for hours. I wasn't doing so well myself that night, so I went off and played video games for an hour or two. I came back to find Ted, still chatting up his ideal lass. I told him I was ready to leave, and since Ted had driven with me, this meant he had to leave, too.

Ted said good-bye to the girl he had just spent three hours talking to, and we headed for the exit. I asked Ted if he had gotten her phone number. He said no—he hadn't had a chance. I stopped in my tracks. I ordered Ted, "Go get her number!" Ted eagerly rushed back to the bar and returned a few moments later, clutching the girl's phone number. They went on to have a short-lived but extremely satisfying relationship that Ted remembers fondly. To this day, he credits me with helping him close the deal. That's what I mean by a little encouragement going a long way.

Another quick example. I was hanging out in a country-western bar with my friend Paul. Paul saw a girl he was extremely attracted to, but there was only one problem—the girl looked just like his brother's wife! Paul was worried about how this would look at family get-togethers. ("Look! Paul's dating a girl who looks just like his brother's wife! What's the story with that?")

I told Paul, "You haven't even spoken to this girl yet, and already you're worried about family get-togethers! Why don't you just talk to her first, and see where it goes from there?" Since Paul was very attracted to her, he decided to give it a shot. They got married last year. I like to think I had a little something to do with it!

And that's the reason I have written this book. I want to help all the Shy Guys out there, give them that little extra push they may need. Shyness is a disease, but it can be cured. I had to do it the hard way—through a long, painful process of self-discovery. Sure, I had some encouragement over the years, but never enough, and never from the people I needed it from the most. My mother was always supportive, but a Shy Guy desperately needs dating advice from his peers or an older male role model, not from his mom.

My primary source for advice on dating was movies and TV. At the age of seventeen, it was quite a revelation for me to receive some dating tips from the movie *Fast Times at Ridgemont High*, in which the slick womanizer, Damone, offers his shy friend, Mark Ratner, a five-point plan for meeting chicks. It goes like this:

1) Never let on how much you like her.
2) Always call the shots.
3) Act like wherever you are, that's the place to be.
4) When ordering food, find out what she wants and then order for the both of you—that's the classy thing to do.
5) This is most important: when it comes to making out, whenever possible, play side one of *Led Zeppelin IV*.

(I'm not sure how important that last one actually is—in the movie, Ratner plays the wrong Led Zep album, and he still gets the girl. So maybe the choice of music really isn't that crucial if the girl really likes you.)

Other than Damone's five-point plan, I was basically on my own. None of my friends dated much, so I couldn't get any pointers from them. I counted instead on the *Happy Days* gang and *Three's Company*'s Jack Tripper to fill in the blanks.

I remember one night when my older brother came back from a movie, I asked him how he and his date liked the flick. He told me, "We didn't exactly watch the movie!"

I had never been more impressed with my brother than at that moment. He had actually gone to the movies and made out with a girl! He had accomplished the kind of miracle that only happens on TV! Sure, that type of thing was a common occurrence for the Fonz, but for it to happen to someone I actually knew . . .

Well, needless to say, it became my life's goal to bring a girl to the movies and swap saliva with her. And I'm proud to say that this is a feat I have since accomplished, on more than one occasion. How many people can say they have achieved their life's dream? I can!

One final memory from childhood. I remember a rather depressing Billy Joel song called "Captain Jack." The song had a lyric about a guy who stayed at home on a Saturday night and masturbated while his sister went out on dates. Well, that pretty much sums up my social life in junior high and high school. I don't know if this is a situation Billy Joel experienced first-hand (no pun intended), but you can tell it was written from *someone's* actual experience. Believe me, it's pretty tough watching your little sister going out on dates while you stay home, spanking the monkey, because you don't have the guts to ask a girl out.

This book is for all the guys who stay home every Saturday night, while their brothers and sisters go out and have fun. You know who you are. There are millions of you out there. You have everything going for you. People tell you that all the time. You may be good-looking and smart and funny and nice, but when it comes to women, you just don't know the score. You're certain the ladies would like you if they got to know you, but that's the problem—you're too shy to make the first move.

It is my sincere hope that those of you reading this book will gain some useful information from it.

No one should have to get all their dating advice from TV and the movies. And no one should have to go through life alone. If the only thing that's stopping you is that you lack confidence, there may still be hope for you.

I had to teach myself how to meet girls. You've got it easy. All you have to do is read the advice that follows. I've approached thousands of girls over the years and received more than my share of rejections. As time went on, I learned which approaches work well for a Shy Guy (for I am still basically a Shy Guy at heart) and which ones don't.

Here's your chance to benefit from my mistakes. Don't let all my rejections be in vain. I took the punches so you don't have to. (To a Shy Guy, there is no greater pain in the world than the sharp sting of rejection—the bitter anguish of expressing your feelings for a girl, only to crash and burn like a World War I bomber!)

Join me as I take you step by step on the path to overcoming your shyness, learning how to approach the girls you are attracted to, finding out where to meet them, and knowing what to say and do afterwards.

I can't guarantee this book will give you the dating prowess of Scott Baio (He's dated all the girls on *Baywatch*, plus Heather Locklear!), but I like to think that, with a little bit of encouragement, maybe you really can ask out that cute girl in the back of your science class . . . or that new receptionist in the office . . . or that pretty girl who's sitting on the next bar stool.

And that's a fine start, wouldn't you say?

Before we begin, you need to ask yourself the following question: What is the worst thing that can happen to a Shy Guy? I mean, the absolute worst thing?

I'll tell you. It's when a girl finds out he likes her. To a Shy Guy, that is like the Black Plague, the Holocaust, and Vietnam, all rolled into one. It is The End of Life as You Know It. It is D-Day. It is a fate worse than death.

Why is it so bad? Because, a Shy Guy tends to build up a lot of walls around himself. He tends to bury himself in his job, his hobby, or his schoolwork. He tends to surround himself with close friends and family—people he feels safe around.

The life of a Shy Guy involves taking no chances, maintaining a predictable, if dull, routine. No matter where he goes or what he does, a Shy Guy wants to feel comfortable. The goal of a Shy Guy is to avoid risks at all costs.

When a girl finds out you like her, the fragile little world of the Shy Guy is shattered. Suddenly, an element of unpredictability has been added. And there goes that safe little routine the Shy Guy has worked so hard to maintain. Now, there is a new element in the Shy Guy's life that he has no control over. And maintaining control is something that is very important to a Shy Guy.

This is one reason why Shy Guys tend to be very private about their emotions. They tend to not be very good at expressing their feelings, and they don't blather on and on about girls they are attracted to.

Shy Guys like to keep up the illusion that they have no interest in the opposite sex, because, in this way, they avoid a lot of awkward questions about their social lives.

Because once people start quizzing a Shy Guy, they want to know everything. Have you ever had a date? Have you ever had sex? Are there any girls you like? Have you ever asked any of them out? Why not?

Each one of these questions is like a kick in the nuts to a Shy Guy. No one should ever be subjected to a line of questioning like this. Because a Shy Guy is seen as lonely and withdrawn, there are do-gooders out there who feel they must get involved and try to "save" the Shy Guy. They make a project out of him. And this usually backfires horribly. It generally has the effect of making the Shy Guy even more withdrawn.

There is really only one thing stopping a Shy Guy from asking out a girl. The girl could say no. That's all there is to it. It's that simple. To a Shy Guy, the thought of being rejected is so unpleasant, he would rather go through life alone than face the possibility of being rejected.

Fear of rejection is an overwhelming force that keeps a Shy Guy paralyzed for most of his life. All it would take is one face-to-face rejection and a Shy Guy could head for a cave and live out the rest of his life as a hermit.

Well, guess what, Shy Guys—there are even worse things that can happen than the girl saying "no!" Such as? Well, she could laugh at you, but that's not likely. (Although if her friends are around, be prepared for a few snickers as you walk away.) She could insult you—also not likely. She could ignore you, which is a common one. If a girl doesn't want to talk to you, all she has to do is walk past you and pretend she doesn't hear you.

To a Shy Guy, this can be as devastating as a rejection. Many Shy Guys see themselves as rulers of their own little world. To have a girl not even acknowledge your existence is quite a blow to one's ego. There goes your image of being King of the World.

One other bad thing that can happen: Another guy can come over and take her away from you. This one happens a lot. Sometimes you'll be talking to a girl, and things seem to be going well, when some other guy comes over—usually a guy she knows—and suddenly you don't exist. Her face will light up, she'll give the guy a big hug and a kiss on the cheek, and suddenly she'll come alive in a way she never was with you.

You may wonder what can be done to avoid any of these fates. Well, the solution is to go on living life like you have been. Stay home every night, never approach any girls, surround yourself with people you feel safe around, never take any chances.

Because if you ever want to meet anyone, you're going to have to take some risks. You're going to have to come out of that asexual closet and admit you have a sex drive. In other words, you're going to have to let people know you like girls.

It's dangerous, I'll admit. A lot of bad things can happen as a result.

Sure, you're opening yourself up to potential rejection, but you know something. It's not that bad.

Most girls have enough tact not to reject you cruelly. Usually they're fairly pleasant about it. Most of them won't laugh in your face. They don't like to be rejected, either, so they can sympathize. Many girls are so good at rejecting guys, it may be days or even weeks before you even realize you've been dissed!

Of course, no matter how gently a girl lets you down, the irrefutable fact is that rejection hurts. It hurts a lot. But you know what? It's not the end of the world. So a girl doesn't want to go out with you. So what? There are a million other girls out there who do. Why waste your time on the one girl who you know you don't have a chance with?

Life's too short to dwell on your failures. If you get shot down, get over it, and move on to the next girl. And if she rejects you, too, then move on to the next one! There's a great big world out there, and if you're not getting as much as you can out of life because fear of rejection is holding you back, then it's time you made some changes.

Picture this scene: You're at a party. You see a cute girl. She makes eye contact with you and smiles. What do you do?

If you're like most Shy Guys, you do absolutely nothing. You wait until she leaves, and then you go home alone, and maybe lie awake in bed, replaying the scene over and over in your mind, thinking of all the things you should have said and done.

When you see a beautiful girl, you want to go over and talk to her, but you can't. It's like there's an invisible wall between you and that girl that's preventing you from talking to her. You can see her, and she can see you, but you have no way of communicating with her. That's why I'm here—to help you get over that invisible wall. But be warned: it's not an easy climb, and you may lose your footing from time to time along the way.

Scaling the wall is one of the most difficult things for a Shy Guy to do. It took me years to do it, and I worked at it full time.

But once you make it over that wall, you will feel better about yourself, and you will have a more fulfilling life. You may find, as you overcome your shyness, that you develop more confidence in every aspect of life and become a more complete person.

Now, I don't expect you to stop being shy all of a sudden. It simply doesn't work that way. Even though I consider myself a reformed Shy Guy, there is still a shy side to my personality that will always be there. Even today, there are situations in which I am uncomfortable meeting new people.

What I'm trying to do is get you to say, "OK, I'm shy. Now, how can I work around that?"

I want you to see that you can meet girls *despite* your shyness, to work with your handicap. There are little tricks I've learned over the years that enable me to meet girls, despite a shyness complex. You may not be comfortable approaching strangers, but you can make the process more comfortable for yourself. The more comfortable you are, the easier it will be.

But first, you have to get over the wall. And the way we do that is by placing you in situations you feel comfortable. I'll teach you to recognize situations where a Shy Guy can excel. In time, you may advance to the point where you're even excelling in non-Shy Guy situations. But we'll worry about that later. For now, let's work on getting over that invisible wall.

Because once you've made it over the wall, your life can truly begin, and you're never going to want to go back to the other side again.

There are ways to suppress shyness, to push it to the back of your mind, so that nobody would ever know you're shy. When people meet me these days, they have a hard time believing I ever had a shy bone in my body. But it's true. Over the course of a few years, I pulled off a near-total transformation, from painfully shy to almost completely fearless.

And you can do it, too. Just because you were born shy doesn't mean you have to die that way. People can change. It is possible. You just have to be willing to make the effort.

Chapter One

Are You a Shy Guy?

This book is designed to help Shy Guys take a one-way trip out of Shy Town and into Confidenceville, USA—population: You! Take the following quiz to determine if you are a Shy Guy, and if this is the right book for you. You may pick more than one response to each question. Give yourself one point for each answer you pick. Then add up the total number of points when you are finished.

1) The thought of meeting a new girl makes you:
   a) enthusiastic for a new opportunity
   b) as tense as Al Gore
   c) paralyzed with fear
   d) tongue-tied

2) Which of the following Warner Brothers characters best describes your social skills?
   a) Pepe Le Pew (smooth Casanova with body odor)

b) Bugs Bunny (hides in a hole most of the time)
c) Foghorn Leghorn (talks the talk, but can't walk the walk)
d) Tasmanian Devil (no focus; all over the place; mildly retarded)
e) Yosemite Sam (loud and blustery, always shooting off his guns)

3) You don't like meeting new people because:
a) you are uncomfortable with your appearance
b) you are afraid you will say the wrong thing
c) you are not particularly good at conversation
d) you are very picky about who you associate with

4) You prefer to:
a) surround yourself with a small group of close friends
b) hang out alone
c) associate only with your family
d) chase after every girl in sight
e) join clubs that have almost exclusively male memberships

5) If you had things your way, you would:
a) go through life celibate
b) have one girl who you could be with for the rest of your life
c) go through more chicks than the Fonz
d) have subscriptions to all the best porno mags

6) When people ask you personal questions about your social life, you wish you could:
a) curl up and die
b) disappear

c) cause them as much humiliation as they are causing you
d) rip their heads off

7) When you meet a girl you like, you:
a) let her know right away
b) keep it to yourself, for fear of embarrassment
c) tell only a few close friends
d) find a way that you can be around her all the time, without actually letting on that you like her

8) The reason you never meet any girls is because:
a) you are so busy with school
b) you are so busy with work
c) you never have any opportunities
d) you just don't know how to talk to girls
e) you are good at making excuses

9) Your idea of a good time is:
a) a quiet night at home, alone, reading a book
b) a quiet night at home, alone, watching TV
c) playing Myst on your computer
d) a night out with the boys, chasing chicks

10) You never have any luck with girls because:
a) you are too picky
b) you are waiting for a girl to approach you
c) you don't try hard enough
d) you are just unlucky in love

11) You do not have a girlfriend because:
a) you don't want one at this time
b) you can't afford one

c) your friends always ruin your chances
d) you are intimidated by the girls you really like
e) you just haven't found the right one yet

12) You are most comfortable talking to:
a) strippers
b) phone sex operators
c) barmaids and waitresses
d) girls at parties

13) The one thing preventing you from dating any girls right now is:
a) you live at home, and your family would only embarrass you
b) your friends would bust your chops
c) you don't make enough money to take anyone out
d) you are really good at making excuses

14) The Elvis Presley song that best sums up your experiences with girls so far is:
a) "Love Me Tender"
b) "Don't Be Cruel"
c) "Heartbreak Hotel"
d) "Kissing Cousins"

15) If a girl found out you liked her, you would:
a) kill yourself
b) consider joining the priesthood
c) become nervous and uncomfortable around her
d) take advantage of this situation

16) When people ask you nosy questions about your personal life, you:

a) pleasantly answer all the questions
b) lie like a rug
c) wish a bolt of lightning would come down and strike them dead
d) politely inform them that it's none of their business

17) The thing that scares you the most is:
a) having your fingernails ripped off one by one
b) having a pit bull chomp onto your genitals and not let go
c) walking around naked in Times Square
d) having a girl find out you like her

18) Which of the following group names did the singing Brady kids perform under on *The Brady Bunch*?
a) The Brady 6
b) The Brady City Rollers
c) The Brady Rhythm Section
d) The Silver Platters

(Okay, I admit, that last question had nothing to do with being shy. I just threw it in to see if you were paying attention. The answers are A and C. But if you were a Shy Guy in the early seventies, you probably spent a lot of Friday nights at home watching *The Brady Bunch*!)

SCORING: 10–15 points: You're not a Shy Guy! What the hell are you doing reading this book?
16–20 points: You're semi-shy, but with a little help, you can be saved.
21–25 points: You're a Shy Guy! You need this book! Study it like the Bible! Memorize it! Learn it! Know it!

26–30 points: To paraphrase Kajagoogoo, you're too shy-shy, hush hush, eye to eye!
31–35 points: Well, at least we've identified your problem. Now let's see what we can do to solve it!
36–40 points: Have you tried that Nintendo 64? They've got some really cool graphics . . .

Okay, so let's say you've taken my little quiz, and you've confirmed what you already knew all along—that you are a Shy Guy. Now what do you do?

Shy Guy Movies to Watch

If there's a recurring theme to this book, it's that we can look to the magic of Hollywood to inspire us in our quest to overcome shyness. One of the oldest Hollywood cliches is that of the nerdy guy who learns how to stand up for himself and become a man. Countless movies have carried this theme. Here's an overview of the ones that do it well. These are the films that you may want to watch to help you pick up a few pointers on your road to Real Manhood.

Night Shift (1982): One of the greatest Shy Guy movies of all time. In a complete reversal from his Fonzie persona, Henry Winkler stars as a mild-mannered nerd who is pushed around by everyone. In an unforgettable debut, Michael Keaton plays a frantic wildman named Billy Blaze—he's energetic, he's funny, he's full of personality. Keaton embarks on a mission to make Winkler into a man. Keaton is the mentor every real-life Shy Guy wishes he had. By the end of the movie, Winkler learns to stand up to the deli delivery boy, talk back to barking dogs, and inspire a hooker to quit hooking and become his girlfriend. This is the movie that redefined the "nerd-into-man" story for our generation.

Risky Business (1983): A classic movie, in the same mode as *Night Shift*. Tom Cruise plays Joel, a high school kid who always strikes out with chicks. At the beginning of the movie, Joel confesses to his friends that he blew a chance to score with a hot girl at his school. Joel's friends mock his awkwardness with girls. Then Joel winds up turning his home into a brothel and taking on the head hooker as his girlfriend. Needless to say, he wins the respect of his friends, who go on to become some of his best customers! Even though his brothel is shut down and all his profits are taken away from him, Joel makes it into Princeton—and still gets to keep the hooker as his girlfriend! Even more important, Joel has learned what it means to be a man. Oh yeah, he also gets to make love on a train!

(Interesting to note how many movies seem to feel a Shy Guy needs a hooker in order to become a man . . . An earlier movie to contain this theme was a 1973 Jack Nicholson flick called *The Last Detail*. In that film, Nicholson is a career sailor ordered to transport a young kleptomaniac to prison. But before that klepto can get to jail, Nicholson makes sure the kid gets drunk, gets in a bar fight, and gets a hooker. This is Hollywood's three-point plan for becoming a man!)

One Flew Over the Cuckoo's Nest (1975): Aside from being one of the greatest movies of all time, this Academy Award–winner also has a great subplot about a Shy Guy. Jack Nicholson plays McMurphy, a convict who pretends to be crazy so he'll be put in an asylum instead of going to prison. One of the inmates he meets in the asylum is Billy, a kid who, at first, seems to have some serious mental problems, but is actually suffering from a bad case of shyness (as well as an overbearing mother complex). McMurphy figures out how to cure Billy's condition—he invites a couple of babes to the insitution for a party! One of the party girls takes a liking to Billy, and the two start to get it on. That wicked Nurse Ratched comes along and breaks up the party and threatens to tell Billy's mother. Billy winds up committing suicide. If only the staff of the institution had let McMurphy implement his rather radical methods of curing shyness, Billy would still be around today.

Hardbodies (1984): This classic teen sex comedy addresses the plight of men who are successful in business, but unlucky in love. What do you do if you've made millions, but still can't get girls? Here we find the answer!

Hardbodies is the story of three middle-aged businessmen—Hunter, Ashby, and Rounder (he's the fat one, natch!)—who move into a California beach house and hire a surfer dude to teach them how to score with chicks! The surfer dude is Scotty, a master at picking up Hardbodies, which, he informs us, are "the perfect little foxes down on the beach." According to Scotty, the way to approach Hardbodies is to "dialogue" them by giving them the BBD—the Bigger, Better Deal. Scotty says, "Chicks want something better out of life. The faster car. The richer boyfriend. The hotter action. That's the BBD." Scotty feels that conventional pickup lines won't work on a Hardbody.

He tells his students, "These chicks are black and blue from guys hitting them with lines. Ya gotta give them them something fresh." Scotty's suggested approach? When you see a pretty girl Rollerblading on the strip, fall down in front of her. Then ask her if she is a model. Tell her, "We're having a party on Saturday, and every modeling agent in the city is gonna be there—and I bet they'd love to meet you!" Scotty notes that "dialoguing" a girl is easy. "Any slob can do it."

Scotty also recommends heading down to the mall, which he calls "a hidden valley of Hardbodies. They're alone, they're off guard, and they're ready to be dialogued!" (This is one point where Scotty is right on target. See the chapter on "The Best Places to Meet Girls"!) Scotty also has the three middle-aged guys get new haircuts and a new wardrobe. Thanks to the advice of Scotty, his three charges succeed in their goal of landing some Hardbodies.

Among the other techniques employed: Hunter spills a drink on a girl's dress, then convinces her to take it off and run some water on it. Then he makes his move! Rounder poses as a photographer and tricks girls into posing topless for him at a party. Ashby serenades a girl with a country-western song he has written based on a line a hooker used to reject Hunter: "I Don't Fuck Fossils for Free!" Another character, a big beach bully, teaches his dog to steal the bikini tops of pretty girls lying on the beach.

Any of these methods seem reasonable to me, especially if you are middle-aged and desperate.

FAST TIMES AT RIDGEMONT HIGH (1982): It's funny how many great coming-of-age movies came out in the early eighties. (They just don't make teen sex comedies any more!) This film has many characters, all of them representing different aspects of high school life. One character fancies himself a ladies' man. He is Damone, who advises not talking to girls, just sending out a lot of attitude instead. Damone says, "The attitude dictates that you don't care whether she cums, lays, stays, or prays. I mean, whatever happens, your toes are still tappin'. And when you've got that . . . then you've got the attitude." I'm not so sure the "Attitude" method works in real life, especially for Shy Guys.

One of the kids in the movie, Rat, is a Shy Guy who likes Jennifer Jason Leigh's character, Stacy. Stacy comes on real strong to Rat, inviting him over her house one night when her parents aren't home. Rat, who is a virgin, panics, makes up a lame excuse, and runs home! Talk about shy! I have a hard time believing any Shy Guy would be so afraid of sex that he would run away from it (maybe they should have gotten that kid a hooker). But the scene does illustrate that some Shy Guys are not comfortable with the idea of sex without love. Every Shy Guy likes to think that his first time is going to be special, that it's going to be with a girl he really cares about. Sadly, it doesn't always work out that way. By the end of the movie, Stacy decides to reverse tactics and pursue Rat the old-fashioned way, by courting him. It is implied that this method will work much better for her, instead of rushing him into something he's just not ready for. (In real life, she probably would have thought Rat was gay and given up on him.)

Other teen sex comedies from the eighties that you may enjoy include *The Last American Virgin, Fraternity Vacation, Valley Girl,* and *Heaven Help Us.*

Back to the Future (1985): The first movie in the trilogy is really the only good one, and for one very significant reason: it is the only one of the three that featured the incomparable Crispin Glover in the role of George McFly, father to Michael J. Fox's Marty. The story has Marty McFly traveling back in time, where he must teach his Shy Guy father how to get over his shyness and ask out the girl who is destined to become his wife (and Marty's mom). Glover does a tremendous job portraying the awkwardness and hesitation of a Shy Guy. Marty has to resort to some desperate methods, such as dressing up like Darth Vader and zapping George with his Walkman. Eventually, George comes around, ending his life of Shyness the old-fashioned way, by giving that mean ol' Biff a punch in the nose. In the end, we see that George McFly's life has turned out for the better. By learning to stand up for himself, he has gone on to become a best-selling author and an aggressive, confident man, instead of a wimp. So the message of the movie can be seen as this: Shy Guys get walked all over. Real Men stand up for themselves.

ROXANNE (1987): *Cyrano de Bergerac* is perhaps the all-time great treatment of the Shy Guy phenomenon, and this movie, written by and starring Steve Martin, is a modern telling of that timeless tale. Martin plays a fireman in love with the beautiful Roxanne, played by Daryl Hannah. Because of his rather prominent snout, Martin is afraid to confess his true feelings. When a better-looking guy asks Martin to help him woo Roxanne, by writing love letters and hiding in the bushes beneath her window and feeding the guy romantic lines to use, Martin agrees. How many Shy Guys out there can relate to being afraid to ask out a girl because you're uncomfortable with your appearance? And how many Shy Guys can relate to watching some other guy make time with the girl who should have been yours? I think we all can.

THE NUTTY PROFESSOR (1963 AND 1996): Whether you prefer Eddie Murphy's remake or the Jerry Lewis original, both movies are about a shy college professor who tries to overcome his condition through chemistry. In Lewis's case, he goes from a skinny nerd to a smooth ladies' man. In Murphy's flick, he goes from a big blubber boy to a svelte stud. Every Shy Guy wishes he could magically transform himself like this—from unconfident weakling who's uncomfortable with his appearance, to cocky Casanova who knows all the right things to say and can get all the girls.

Unfortunately, it doesn't work that way in real life. There are no magic potions you can take to transform yourself. If you really want to change your behavior or your appearance, you're going to have to do both the hard way. For what it's worth, in both movies, the main character finds that easy answers and quick changes are not the solution. Both Murphy and Lewis come to resent what they turn into, and both are happy to go back to the way they were.

BIG (1988): This beloved Tom Hanks film offers an insightful look at how a little boy's shyness can carry over into adulthood. The film tells the story of a young boy who magically becomes an adult overnight, but still has the mind of a child. A lot of Shy Guys can relate to this, because many Shy Guys are just children in grown-up bodies. There are times when I still feel as shy as I did when I was five years old.

In this film, Hanks's character is very naive sexually. When he excitedly tells a girl, "I get to be on top!" he's talking about bunk beds, not sex positions. When the woman finally decides to have sex with Hanks, she finds she must be the aggressor. This is a situation every Shy Guy can relate to. If women never made the first move when it comes to lovemaking, many Shy Guys would still be virgins.

Another good Hanks movie about a Shy Guy is *Forrest Gump*. Technically, Forrest is really more of a semi-retarded guy than a Shy Guy, but still, he is very timid when it comes to putting the moves on his true love, Jenny. Forrest even experiences premature ejaculation, and that's something every Shy Guy can relate to, I'm sure! (Not that I would know anything about that . . .)

SWINGERS (1996): *Swingers* is a low-budget movie that offers a very funny look at a bunch of pickup artists and their various techniques. One of the Swingers is a Shy Guy who is still pining for his ex-girlfriend six months after their breakup. The other Swingers try to help the Shy Guy overcome his funk and get on with his life.

In one hilarious scene, the Shy Guy gets a girl's phone number—and then makes the biggest mistake you can make: he calls her the *same night* and leaves four messages on her answering machine! Needless to say, the girl never wants to see him again!

A good film to study for technique, even if some of the pickups are a little unbelievable.

Pretty Woman (1991): In this film, Richard Gere plays a high-powered executive who is in LA for a few days on business and needs a female companion to attend some social functions with him. Since he doesn't have a girlfriend, Gere decides to hire a hooker (naturally)!

When he sees a streetwalker (played by Julia Roberts) on the corner, Gere's character asks her for directions! The filmmakers try to make Gere appear more sympathetic here by making it seem like Gere is really lost, and would never even think about approaching a hooker. But us Shy Guys know the truth: Gere wasn't really lost. He only asked for directions as an excuse to talk to the hooker! Fortunately for him, Roberts is an aggressive hooker, and she closes the deal.

After one weekend together, Roberts falls in love with Gere, gives up her life of prositution for him, and they go off to get married. That must make for some interesting stories at cocktail parties. "So, how did you two meet, anyway?"

Milk Money (1995): This movie deals with a kid who lives with his widowed father, played by Ed Harris. Since the kid knows his father is too shy to ever meet another woman, the kid does what any loving son would do. He saves up his milk money and hires his dad a hooker (played by Melanie Griffith)! I can only hope that someday my children love me enough to do the same for me!

Naturally, by the end of the movie, Melanie has fallen in love with Ed, given up hooking, and agreed to marry him! Hollywood seems to have this real fascination with the idea that it's okay for a Shy Guy to use a hooker to help him get over his shyness, as long as the hooker turns into an Honest Woman in the end. Well, whatever works . . .

Shy Guys on TV

Since Shy Guys generally spend over half their lives at home watching TV, we'll finish this chapter with a look at TV Shy Guys.

For every Fonzie, there is a Potsie. For every Vinnie Barbarino, there is an Arnold Horshack. The TV landscape has always been littered with Shy Guys who seek out the advice of Cool Guys who know how to score. Unfortunately, in real life, Shy Guys often lack helpful role models. Not all of us have a tough-but-cool friend who dispenses advice on meeting girls.

No, most Shy Guys have to do it on their own. They're usually too shy to consult with other Shy Guys, so they can't even take comfort in the knowledge that others are suffering as they are.

In the event that you can't find a real-life Fonzie, you may just want to be inspired by the examples you see on TV. Here's my round-up of some famous TV Shy Guys.

Richie Cunningham: Richie was your basic awkward teenager, but he was fortunate in that he had his horny friend, Potsie, who pushed him into getting into all kinds of trouble. Although Potsie was a bad influence, he never asked Richie to do anything that was *really* bad. When Richie looks back on his high school experience, the things he will remember most fondly are the things he did with Potsie. Like the time they got fake IDs and snuck into a strip club. Like the time they got in a drag race. Like the time they almost joined a street gang.

Although Richie was initially reluctant to do any of these things (a Shy Guy never wants to break the law or go against the rules), he could be talked into almost anything. That's pretty much the way it works in real life. Usually a Shy Guy's first impulse is to turn down any invitation to do anything different. Speaking from personal experience, I can say that my first impulse is to say "no" whenever anyone asks me to do anything I haven't done before. Why would I want to do something different? What happens if I don't like it? No, it's safer just to stay home and follow the old reliable routine.

That's the Shy Guy way.

But if TV has taught us nothing else, it's that the greater you resist doing something ("Uh-uh! I am not going hang gliding! No way! No how!"), the more fun you will have when you finally give in and do it. ("Look at me! I'm hang gliding! Wheeee!")

We all need a Potsie in our lives. Every responsible person needs an irresponsible sidekick to lead them into all kinds of mischief. Without that rascally sidekick, our lives would be a lot less interesting.

Let me give you a real-life example of the Potsie Syndrome. My friend Patrick had been dumped by his girlfriend of several years, and he was taking it hard. He went into a deep depression; he spent his nights walking the streets in the rain, crying. He had basically sunk about as low as a human being could go.

He just couldn't let go of his ex-girlfriend. She had gone on with her life, met a new guy, but Pat was having a real hard time starting over. He couldn't get her off his mind.

One night, me and my buddy Dave were going on a road trip to a new nightclub we had heard about. We invited Pat to come with us. He turned us down, saying he wasn't interested. We badgered him, cajoled him, and pressured him, until finally, he caved in and agreed to come along, swearing he was not going to have any fun.

We went to the nightclub, and Patrick met a girl—a cute nanny. After the club closed, Patrick and the nanny went to a diner for a bite to eat. Then they started dating. From there, Patrick's confidence grew so much that he started asking out other girls. The next thing you knew, he was dating two girls at once!

He rebounded big time from his earlier funk. It was one of the healthiest recoveries from a breakup I had ever seen, and it all came about because we had badgered Pat to come out with us that night. It just goes to show you the importance of being supportive to your friends.

It would be great if we all knew a seemingly-dangerous-but-really-harmless biker who could dispense all his wisdom in the art of dating, but realistically, that's probably not going to happen. More likely, we'll have to rely on our fellow Shy Guys for support. So if you have a mischievous friend who's always trying to get you to do stuff that goes against your Shy Guy nature, why not give it a try sometime? Likewise, you should try to support your friends in all their wacky adventures. (Just try to stay away from those drag races!)

Ross Geller: This character from the TV series *Friends* is the perfect example of the Shy Guy who wastes half his life pining over a girl before finally revealing his true feelings to her. Ever since he was in high school, Ross had the hots for Rachel, who was his sister's best friend. But Ross never acted on his feelings. Instead, he admired Rachel from afar, pining for her, dreaming of her, but never daring to express how he really felt.

Because of Ross's shyness, he almost let Rachel slip through his fingers. He could only stand by helplessly as she announced her engagement to another man.

Fortunately, Rachel's wedding plans fell apart and he got another chance. That's something a lot of guys don't get. Even after Rachel called off her engagement, Ross was afraid to pounce. (As we'll discuss later, Shy Guys don't pounce!) It was another full year before Rachel found out Ross liked her! By then, Ross was in another relationship with someone else.

Eventually, things worked out and Ross and Rachel finally got together, but it took far longer than it should have. Just think if Ross had told Rachel how he felt about her when they were both in high school. Think of all the great times they could have had together. They could have gone to the prom together, been dating all through college—they could have had another ten years together! Instead, Rachel was out having fun, while Ross spent all his time moping and making puppy-dog eyes.

Because of his Shyness, Ross wasted years of his life. Any Shy Guy can relate to that. Just about every Shy Guy knows what it's like to have a big crush on the girl next door, only to go your whole life without ever seeing it consummated.

Don't make the same mistake Ross made. Don't wait ten years to tell a girl how you really feel. Tell her today. If there's one thing the TV show *Friends* has taught us it's that it's never too late for a man and a woman who are friends to become lovers. (Even though Ross and Rachel eventually broke up, at least they had a season and a half together! And you know they are destined to get back together again. My prediction: they'll be married years from now, when the show reaches its last episode!)

RADAR O'REILLY: This Shy Guy from the TV series *M*A*S*H* suffered through eight years of the Korean War (which, as we all know, really only lasted two and half years), with only a small handful of dates to his credit. All around him, irresponsible doctors and soldiers were cheating on their wives, going into town to get hookers, and chasing nurses. Radar could only sit back and watch as the camp studs, Hawkeye and Trapper John scored on a nightly basis. Even though Radar was a nice guy with good intentions, he couldn't help but feel a little envious of the dating prowess of the doctors in "The Swamp."

On those rare occasions when Radar could actually get a date, he would always turn to Hawkeye and Trapper for advice. In one instance, Radar was dating a sophisticated girl who had an interest in classical music. Radar felt out of his element. How could a naive Iowa farmboy possibly hope to impress such a girl?

Good ol' Hawkeye came through with the answer. He told Radar, "Whenever she talks about classical music, just say, 'Aaaaah . . . Bach." Radar tried it and unfortunately the line didn't work, but Hawkeye came to the rescue yet again, piping in with, "I guess once you've said, 'Aaaah, Bach,' there's nothing more left to say!"

Even though Radar was stationed alongside the studly surgeons for the duration of the Korean War, he really didn't take advantage of their advice on dating as much as he could have. When he got his orders and went back home to Ottumwa, Iowa, he packed up his teddy bear and his grape Nehis and left behind a golden opportunity to learn about the ladies.

For all his ability to predict the future, there was one thing Radar's psychic powers couldn't do, and that's read the hearts and minds of the women around him. If he had learned to do this, his Shy Guy days would have been behind him forever!

Cliff Clavin: Cliff (from *Cheers*) represents an extreme version of a Shy Guy. He's the classic example of the guy who thinks he knows everything about everything, but knows nothing when it comes to women. Whenever he tries to talk to a pretty girl, Cliff gets so tongue-tied he can't even form words. Only nonsense sounds come out of his mouth. Yet if you ask him about the history of the Pony Express, he'll bore you for hours with endless stories.

This is the kind of guy you see a lot of in bars. Guys who are incredibly knowledgeable when it comes to certain subjects—usually sports and cars—but know absolutely zilch about women. Back in my bartending days, it always amazed me how some guys could be so confident when it came to certain subjects, yet so terrified of girls. Why couldn't they take that confidence they had in every other aspect of life and apply it to the opposite sex?

Cliff spent eleven years sitting on the bar stool at Cheers, and if the show hadn't been cancelled, he'd still be there today. Cliff had a couple of dates over the course of the show's run, but he usually botched them by making a blithering idiot of himself. If you see yourself as a real-life Cliff Clavin, you may want to return this book, because I'm afraid there may be no hope for you!

JOHN BURNS: (*Taxi*) John was the Shy Guy who appeared in the first season of *Taxi*, and then disappeared and was never referred to again. He occupies a special place in TV history, along with Spearchucker and Ugly John from *M*A*S*H* and Richie Cunningham's older brother, Chuck, from *Happy Days*—characters who disappeared and were forgotten, as if they had never existed.

The only storyline of his own John ever had was one episode when he was looking for a good pickup line. He decided to try, "Will you marry me?" Much to his surprise, it actually worked. A girl John met in a bar said yes, and John was stuck marrying her. Yeah, like that would happen! If you ever tried to use this line in real life, the girl would think you were a desperate loser and she would never, ever say yes. (Or if she did, she would be joking!)

I guess the lesson to be learned here is that what works on TV doesn't always work in real life.

There's nothing wrong with picking a TV character from one of your favorite shows and trying to emulate him. But set realistic goals. We can't all be Fonzie.

Pick a TV character that you can actually relate to. For instance, when I was growing up, I always wanted to be one of the Monkees, preferably Mickey—the funny one. The Monkees had the life. They lived in an awesome house on the beach with a cool car, they had pretty girls coming over all the time, and they got chased by monsters and gangsters. It doesn't get any better than that! At least there was a chance of me actually having a life like Mickey's, except for the part about the monsters.

Da-Wayne (*What's Happenin'*!!): *The Complete Directory to Prime Time Network and Cable TV Shows* describes Da-Wayne as "the shy tagalong, always striving to be 'cool.' " He's a classic Shy Guy. When he walked into a room, he was full of confidence, greeting his friends with a hearty "Hey Hey Hey!" But when it came to girls, Da-Wayne was quiet and reserved. Perhaps he felt a little intimidated, hanging out with his smart pal, Raj, and the flamboyant Rerun, whose colorful wardrobe and energetic dancing would always capture the crowd's attention. When competing with guys like that, Da-Wayne would be lucky to get a date with fat Shirley the waitress!

Of course, since he was a sitcom character, Da-Wayne still did much better than a real-life Shy Guy would have. He could always get a date to the Doobie Brothers concert if he needed one. As you may have noticed, characters on TV sitcoms do quite a bit of dating. There is a lot we can learn from their methods. Whenever you're not sure what to say to a girl, just say to yourself, "What would Schneider from *One Day at a Time* do in this situation?"

If it means disguising yourself as a woman and moving into an all-girl hotel in order to win the girl you love, then so be it. If it means pretending to be gay to fool your landlord so you can move in with two sexy roommates (well, okay, one sexy roommate and her sensible friend), then go for it. As TV has taught us, no approach is too outrageous. There's no such thing as going too far when pursuing your soulmate—even if you have to steal her away from her snooty rich fiancé on their wedding day.

Some of these approaches may seem a bit extreme, but for all its razzle-dazzle, Hollywood does try to inspire us to do better. If we follow the examples set by our favorite movie and TV characters, we can't lose. If nothing else, we can borrow from these characters their persistence and their incredible optimism.

Now that we have identified all the different types of Shy Guys on TV, and witnessed Shy Guys transforming into real men in the movies, it's time to teach you about actually getting out there and meeting girls.

Chapter Two

The Best and Worst Opening Lines

"I hate using lines! I could never use a line on a girl!"

This is something every Shy Guy says at one time or another. A Shy Guy likes to think he is creative, unique, individual. By using a common "pickup line," a Shy Guy is admitting he is the same as all those other chumps out there, and no Shy Guy wants to admit that. Better to stay alone and clever, than to be common and have a girlfriend!

There is a great Billy Joel song about singles bars called "Sleeping With The Television On." The premise of the song is that men and women go out to singles bars hoping to meet someone, but are too scared to connect with each other, so they wind up going home alone and falling asleep with the TV on. The song speaks of a guy who is so afraid of using somebody else's line that he instead chooses to say nothing.

This sums up the Shy Guy philosophy in a nutshell. A Shy

Guy refuses to use a line because somebody else may have used it before. And a Shy Guy is much too clever and imaginative to do that! There is a word for this kind of thinking: "cop-out." Basically, a Shy Guy will look for any excuse not to talk to a girl. Wanting to avoid cliches and tired old pickup lines gives the Shy Guy just the rationalization he needs for not making an effort.

At the end of the night, as he goes home alone again for the millionth time, the Shy Guy can tell himself, "Well, at least I didn't use any of those tired old lines I heard all the other guys using!" (Meanwhile, all those other guys are getting phone numbers and taking girls home!)

Let me tell you something about opening lines. They are a necessary part of the dating experience. All they really are is icebreakers—a way of initiating conversation with someone you are attracted to.

Ultimately, whatever opening line you use is meaningless, because if a girl is attracted to you, she will keep talking to you no matter what your opening line is. You can have the most awkward introduction in the world, but if a girl likes you, she'll overlook a bumpy start. She may even find your nervousness cute and endearing!

All that really matters is that you break the ice. Once you've established contact with a girl, you'll be amazed at how easily the rest comes. You'll find there are plenty of girls out there who really want to talk to you. But you have to be the one to start the conversation. In our male-dominated society, it is customary for the man to make the first move.

Here is where we realize just how much harder it is for guys to meet someone than it is for girls. If a girl wants to let men know she is available, all she has to do is leave the house. The simple fact that she has gone out in public sends a signal to men that she is available. The sad fact is that almost any girl in the world can have any guy she wants just by saying one word to him: "Hello." That's all it takes for a girl to break the ice. But for guys, the ice is much thicker and harder, and may require some sort of high-powered drill to cut through.

It is not easy for a Shy Guy to strike up conversations with strangers, so it is often necessary to rely on an opening line, just to get the girl's attention. But there are good opening lines that actually are effective, and there are bad ones that turn a girl off completely.

Using a cliched old line like "What's your sign?" is a waste of time and doesn't accomplish anything. But if you ask a girl a harmless question that doesn't sound like a line from a seventies sitcom, it is much easier to launch a conversation.

An effective technique is to put yourself in the role of Clueless Boy. Pretend that you need some piece of information that the girl can easily give you. It doesn't matter whether you really need the information or if you already know the answer to the question. What matters is that the girl thinks you need the information, and her willingness to give it to you will help you determine if she is interested or not.

In order for a Shy Guy to come on to a girl, he must first convince himself that he is not really coming on to her—that he is just requesting some information. In this way, if the girl blows you off, she hasn't really rejected you, because you're not really hitting on her, and this lessens the sting a little bit.

Example: You pretend that you are new in town and would like some information on popular nightclubs in the area. The girl rattles off the names of a few local hot spots, then turns her back on you. Have you been rejected? No, because you didn't really ask her out. You were just asking for some simple information. Once she provided the info, she felt she had done her part, and she felt the conversation was over.

Now, if the girl had liked you, she would most likely have kept the conversation going. Sometimes, the girl will even tell you the name of a club she and her friends are going to, and will invite you and your friends to join her. If you get an invitation, it usually means the girl is interested.

The amazing thing is that a lot of times when you approach a girl and ask her a question, she doesn't realize you are actually coming on to her! She thinks you actually need the information. This works to your advantage. It gives the Shy Guy just the edge he needs to succeed. It's like going hunting for an antelope that doesn't know you are carrying a gun.

Asking a girl about nightclubs works particularly well if you are on vacation, or have recently moved to a new town. It can be less effective if you are in your hometown, where you've spent the past twenty-five years.

I grew up in a small town in New Jersey and lived there for over twenty-five years. Yet there were times when my friends and I would walk up to girls in a local bar and ask them where some good nightclubs were. This puts you in a new category, which is beyond Clueless Boy. I call this category "Retarded Boy," because you would have to be retarded not to know where the nightclubs are in your own town!

Still, girls usually proved willing to help. In these situations, the girl usually catches on real quick that you didn't really need the information she was providing, so you may want to have a good explanation ready as to why you know so little about your hometown. (Maybe you've been so busy with work or school you haven't gone out much lately; maybe you just broke up with a long-term girlfriend and hadn't gone out much; maybe you recently moved back to the area, etc.)

As you can see, a Shy Guy will use any excuse to create the illusion that he is in need of some information and needs an attractive girl to come to his aid.

In an informal survey, most girls say the opening line that

works best on them is "Excuse me, do you have the time?" This line works because you are requesting a very small piece of information that only takes two seconds to give. If she likes you, she can talk to you. But if she's not interested, you only stole a moment of her time.

The bad thing about this line is that it doesn't allow for easy follow-through. Once she's given you the time, your conversation is essentially over, unless you can quickly come up with a new topic of conversation. You have to be fast on your feet, and that's something Shy Guys are not famous for. If you plan on using "What time is it?" as your opening line, you'd better have your follow-up line prepared before you even approach the girl, otherwise you'll be dead in the water.

Somewhat more effective lines deal with the specific setting that you're in. If you're in a club, any of the following will do: "Do you know what time this club closes?" "What time does the band go on?" "Do you know the name of the band?" (Even if there is a giant sign on the wall with the name of the band on it, ask this one anyway. For that matter, even if you are wearing a watch, don't let that stop you from asking a girl for the time. If she notices you have a watch, tell her you need the *correct* time.)

These are all innocuous questions that lend themselves well to further conversation. If there is a band playing, ask her how she likes the music. If she doesn't like the band, ask her what kind of music she does like. If she doesn't like the club she's in, ask her what clubs she does like. Be careful not to ask too many questions. Remember, this is supposed to be a conversation, not an interview.

I like to use what I call the Letterman Rule. Basically, there are three questions David Letterman asks every noncelebrity he interviews:

1) what's your name?
2) where are you from? and
3) what do you do for a living?

Those are all the questions you need to ask a girl you are chatting up. After you've asked her those three questions, she should then throw one of them back at you, asking what *your* name is and what *you* do for a living.

It all comes down to this: If a girl is interested in you, she will ask you questions about yourself. If she is not interested, she will not ask any questions. Got that? It's quite simple, really. There's no room for debate on this. She likes you, you get questions. No like, no questions.

After you've asked your three questions, you don't want to ask her anything else, because girls are turned off by guys who are too inquisitive. At this point, you may want to offer some information about yourself and see if she is paying attention. Tell her your name, and where you're from, even if she doesn't ask. Some girls are intimidated by strange men approaching them, so you may have to work a little bit to get her to open up to you. Sometimes a girl has to get to know you a little bit before she warms to you.

People who are good conversationalists generally just talk about themselves. This is a good pattern for you to follow. Simply talk about yourself. In doing so, you may get her to offer information about herself, or she might ask you more questions about your own life, which implies she has a strong interest.

Talk about places you usually go and what kind of music you like. If you had an interesting adventure on the way to the club, tell her about it. If you are going someplace interesting later on, let her know. You have to go into a conversation with the assumption that everything about your life is interesting.

There was a great *Calvin and Hobbes* comic strip in which

Calvin gave his thoughts about conversation. He said, "You know what I hate? I hate when I'm talking and someone turns the conversation to himself! It's so rude! Why do they think I'm talking? It's so they can hear about *me*! Who cares what *they* have to say? If I start a conversation, it should stay on the subject of *me*!"

Now, while Calvin's methods of conversation domination may be a little extreme, he does have a point. At the very least, you want to hold your own in a conversation. You don't want the girl to dominate it. You want to come across as a well-rounded individual who has a fascinating life. She'll never know how fascinating you are unless you open your mouth and tell her! I've generally found that people will babble on about their own lives unless you interrupt them by babbling on about your life. I like to use what I call the Pre-emptive Strike method of conversation. The philosophy behind it is this: I'm gonna bore you with trivial details about my life before you have the chance to bore me!

If all you're doing is asking a girl about her life, then all you're really doing is stroking her ego. You want to come across as an equal, not a sycophant. You want the two of you to be on roughly the same level, if possible. If one of you is more interested in the other, the conversation can be a little one-sided.

I find you can tell a lot about someone by inquiring about the type of places they hang out and the type of music they listen to. If the girl likes country-western bars and you like rock clubs, maybe this is not the girl for you. If you like dance clubs and she likes sleazy pool halls, this is probably not a relationship worth pursuing. If you like sports bars and she likes freaky alternative clubs, don't waste your time.

Forget all that nonsense you've heard about opposites attracting. With only rare exceptions, the opposite is true: opposites repel, and they do so with extreme prejudice.

Another thing I like to do fairly early on in the conversation is to find out what the girl is into. What are her hobbies? Does she play any sports? I like to find out if the girl likes movies. I enjoy going to the movies and renting videos. If a girl tells me she hates movies, this is not someone I want to spend too much time with. I usually find that within a few minutes of conversation about local clubs, movies, and music, I can tell if I have any future with a girl.

One thing I learned early on is that every girl likes a compliment. Girls often spend hours getting ready before they go out, so a small compliment from you is greatly appreciated. It serves as an acknowledgment that her efforts have paid off. As Homer Simpson once said, "When it comes to compliments, women are ravenous, bloodsucking monsters, always wanting more, more, *more*! And if you give it to them, you get plenty back in return!"

What I like to do is focus on one feature that I find particularly attractive about her. "That's a very pretty dress." "You have the most beautiful eyes!" "You've got great hair!" These are compliments that work pretty well.

One thing to keep in mind, though: If a girl does have, for example, incredible hair, she's probably had a million guys tell her so. You may be the tenth guy today who's told her how nice her hair is.

After a while, she begins to resent that the only thing people seem to notice about her is her hair. In this case, you may want to find something else to comment on—something that maybe nobody else would notice. "That's a really interesting pendant. Where did you get it?" Something like that. There may be an interesting story behind where a girl got a particular piece of jewelry. Maybe she got it while on a vacation in a fascinating, far-off city. Maybe it was a gift from her aunt. Sometimes there isn't any story, though, and the girl just answers, "I got it at Sears," and the conversation ends.

When using the compliment line, again, it is often necessary to have a backup line ready, after you've given the compliment. It is generally up to you to keep the conversation flowing at this point, to let the girl know you're interested in talking to her beyond simply complimenting her. Often, the girl is oblivious. She thinks you just came over to compliment her, and that's it. So it's up to you to turn that compliment into a conversation.

Other good icebreakers: comment on how pleasant you find a girl's perfume and ask her which brand it is. Another good one: if you hear a girl speaking with an interesting accent, try to guess what kind of accent she has and ask her if you are correct. If you are in a restaurant and she is eating at the table next to you, ask her what she is eating and if she would recommend it.

These days, many girls have tattoos and interesting body piercings, which provide an easy opening for conversation. You can say to a girl, "That's an awesome tattoo. Where did you get it?" You may even pretend that you're interested in getting a "tat" yourself. Often the tattoo a girl chooses has some special significance to her life, so you can ask why she chose that particular design.

Another possibility: if a girl has her arm in a cast, ask her what happened. There may be an interesting story there. But be careful. I once had a friend who saw a beautiful girl with only one flaw—a big scar on her leg. My friend asked the girl, "How did you get that scar on your leg?" The girl responded, "I was in a car accident. I went through the windshield and had to have my face sewn back together. My best friend died."

Needless to say, my friend didn't get her number. You've got to use a little sensitivity in these situations.

If it sounds like a lot of preparation goes into opening lines, it does. Your opening line may be the one chance you have to get a girl's attention. Once you have it, it's up to you to make sure you keep it. Because after she walks away, that's it. It's over, and you may not get another shot.

A lot of guys find they need a few drinks in them before they can approach girls. I'm not a drinker, myself, but I've been told a couple of beers can help loosen you up. If you have to get your courage from a bottle, that's okay, as long as you don't overdo it.

Another suggestion for a good pickup line is the first one I ever used: "Is your name Kelly?" (Or, as I call it, the old Mistaken Identity Ploy.) The Mistaken Identity Ploy is the oldest pickup line known to man. And you know what? It still works! What you do is walk up to a strange girl and insist that you know her from somewhere. Ask her where she works, where she goes to school. Stand by your claim that you remember her from somewhere, but you just can't recall where. The whole time, you're actually pumping her for information about herself.

The reason this technique works so well for a Shy Guy is because you give yourself an easy out. If, in quizzing the girl about herself you can tell she's not interested in you, or not really your type, you can end the conversation at any time by saying, "I'm sorry, I must have had you mixed up with someone else," and walking away!

Basically, if things are not going well, you can abort the attempted pickup without having been rejected. Any time a Shy Guy can avoid a rejection, it's a good thing. Each rejection lowers a Shy Guy's self-esteem a little more, and makes it that much harder to approach the next girl.

You want to put yourself in situations where at any moment, you can walk away with your dignity intact, leaving the girl unaware that you have just been coming on to her. (Of course, most girls are fully aware of what you're doing, but it is important for a Shy Guy to convince himself that he is being clever.)

The worst pickup lines are those that are either overused, try too hard to be clever, or make it painfully obvious that you are hitting on her. Remember, a Shy Guy must be subtle. You want to create the illusion that you're just a friendly guy, making conversation. You're not one of those slick pickup artists that girls are so repulsed by.

Bearing that in mind, here is my list of the best and worst pickup lines.

TEN BEST PICKUP LINES

1) Do you have the time?
2) What time is this club open until?
3) What's the name of the band?
4) What time does the band come on? (Or, if the band has just gone off, "Do you know if the band is coming back on?")
5) (In a busy club) Is this place always this crowded?
6) (On a slow night) Is it always this quiet in here? (A good follow-up line is, "Which are the best nights to come here?")
7) I'm new in town. Do you know any good clubs in the area?
8) Is your name Kelly?
9) That's a very pretty dress you're wearing.
10) Me and my friend are shooting pool. Would you like to join us in a game? (Other good bar games to play: darts, shuffleboard, video sex trivia.) If the bar offers karaoke, ask her to sing a duet with you. This is a fun, nonthreatening thing two strangers can do together.

A few more good ones: if there is a DJ playing, ask, "Do you know who sings this song?" Another favorite of mine is to fake an imaginary bet with your friend. "My friend says your boots are leather. I say they're snakeskin. Who's right?" If there is a sporting event on TV, ask the girl who is winning. You can gauge her interest in sports by her response, and determine if you have anything in common with her.

Another good approach is to use Shared Experience whenever possible. If there is something happening in a bar that all the customers are watching, ask the girl about it. If the bar is sponsoring some sort of promotion, ask her what it is. If a fight just broke out, ask her what happened. If some cops and an ambulance just left, ask her, "What's the story?" Chances are, the girl has no more idea of what's going on than anybody else in the bar, but that's not the point. Remember, you are Clueless Boy, and she is Information Girl, so it is only natural that you speak to her. If you see a wild bachelorette party going on, pull aside one of the girls in the party and ask her what the celebration is all about. (Dutter's Rule: If you see five or more girls in a nightclub sitting together, nine times out of ten it is a bachelorette party. Dutter's Other Rule: If one of the girls is wearing a bridal veil, it's *definitely* a bachelorette party!)

I find it usually helps to be funny. Everyone likes to laugh, so if you can make a girl smile when you first meet her, she will assume you are a fun person to be around. Sometimes you will meet a girl who completely does not get your sense of humor, but that's okay—there are plenty of other girls out there who will.

I know one Shy Guy who has perfected a technique where he clowns around with his friends in a bar, saying something just loud enough that some nearby girls can hear him. I call this technique the Clown Technique. It can work, if you are funny enough and loud enough. If the girls think my friend is funny, they may acknowledge him. The brilliance of this manuever is that it has eliminated the need for an opening line completely. As a Shy Guy, you want to keep the introduction process as painless and risk-free as possible.

Another Shy Guy I know takes the Clown Technique one step

further, playing the role of Immature Boy. What he will do is crumple up some bar napkins and pretend to throw them at his friends, "accidentally" missing his friends and hitting a girl standing nearby. When the girl turns around, Immature Boy apologizes and then offers to buy her a drink. I can't really recommend this approach, since most girls frown on sophomoric displays of immaturity, but I suppose if you really are a sophomoric person, it is okay. Just try to outgrow it at some point, and work at developing social skills that don't involve throwing stuff.

Sometimes you'll see a girl in a bar who looks like she is having a miserable time. This is a golden opportunity for you. Ask her if she is having a good time and, if not, why not. It could be that the girl is just having a bad night and meeting you could be the thing that turns her night around. In fact, I will often seek out the one girl in a bar who looks like she is having the worst time. I consider it a challenge to try to get her to smile.

Sometimes you meet a girl who just doesn't want to be bothered and is annoyed that you are even talking to her. In these cases, the best thing to do is just turn it into a big joke. Say to her, "Don't you hate it when total strangers come up and start talking to you?" You may want to add, "You meet a lot of phonies in this place," or "This place is such a meat market!" Then turn and walk away. Hey, this stuff is supposed to be fun, kids! And you never know—with the right attitude, you may even turn a rejection into an acceptance.

A couple of other good ones: if you are a smoker, ask a girl for a cigarette or a light. Although I am not a smoker, personally, I must admit cigarettes are the single greatest way to bring two strangers together—at least for a few seconds.

You may want to go with the total honesty approach. A lot of Shy Guys have had great success with this one. You walk up to a girl and say, "Listen, I'm no good with lines, but I find you very attractive and I'd like to get to know you better." This line is pretty bold, and it may take a while for you to work up to it. It won't work every time, but those girls who like it will like it a lot. Anytime you can be honest instead of using some hackneyed old line, it's to your benefit. Most Shy Guys find this approach a little forward. It shatters your illusion of being a friendly, asexual guy, and doesn't leave much of an escape route if the girl is not interested.

I suppose it goes without saying that the greatest opening line of all is "Hi, how are you?" but it usually takes a Shy Guy years to work up to that one. I'm trying to give you the easy ones to start with.

Although there are millions of bad pickup lines, here are some of the worst.

TEN WORST PICKUP LINES

1) What's your sign? (Too seventies. Likewise, "Read any good books lately"—it may have worked on *The Love Boat*, but these are more sophisticated times we live in!)
2) Do you come here often? (Too closely associated with pickup artists. Often a girl will ask you this question, because she wants to determine if you cruise bars a lot. Be very careful answering this question. A girl really doesn't want to hear, "Oh yeah, I'm here every Friday and Saturday night!" They prefer to hear, "I hardly ever go to clubs.")
3) Would you like to dance? (Most girls have no interest in dancing with strangers. Unless you're a phenomenal dancer, your best bet is to get to know her first and then wait until much later in the evening before asking her to dance.)
4) I've been watching you all night and I'd really like

to get to know you. (Too stalkerish; you don't want to scare the girl away before you've even met her.)

5) My friend thinks you're really cute and wants to meet you. (Girls hate this line, because it implies that a] your friend is a coward, and b] you have no interest in her yourself.]
6) Will you marry me? (Too cutesy for an opening line; only works on TV.)
7) If I told you you had a beautiful body, would you hold it against me? (Too *Benny Hill*.)
8) You must be awful tired, because you were running through my dreams all night. (Sounds too much like you were masturbating over her.)
9) You must be a thief, because you stole my heart. (Too corny.)
10) You look just like Cindy Crawford (or some other celebrity.)

Girls *really* don't like being compared to celebrities, even if it is intended as a compliment. Chances are she's been told this by a million guys before and is sick of hearing it. A better bet is to be more creative, tell her she looks like some celebrity that she bears no resemblance to at all. Ask a blonde, blue-eyed girl, "Has anyone ever told you you look like Whoopi Goldberg?" Hopefully the girl has a sense of humor.

Another danger of the celebrity comparison is that a lot of times, you're comparing a girl to a celebrity she finds repulsive. You may tell a girl, "You look just like Brooke Shields," and mean it as a compliment, but she may be horribly offended. I used to date a girl who looked a lot like Kirstie Alley from *Cheers*, but this girl considered Kirstie Alley hideous. She got very offended whenever anybody made the Kirstie Alley comparison. (Hey, at least nobody said she looked like Carla!)

If you feel you must make a celebrity comparison, have the girl make it for you. Ask her, "Which celebrity do people tell you you look like?" You may get some surprising and fun answers. Then ask her which celebrity she thinks you resemble. This is a great icebreaker.

I find that pop culture, in general, works pretty well as a way of bringing two strangers together. We have a very multimedia-literate generation growing up out there. Ask her if she's more of a Brady person or a Partridge person. Ask her to name her favorite seventies disco song. Ask her if she thinks Jeannie from *I Dream of Jeannie* has more powerful magic than Samantha from *Bewitched*. This ties in with my theory of Shared Experience. Many people grew up watching the same TV shows and movies and listening to the same songs. You can use those influences to your advantage. You may have never met someone before, but if you make the right pop culture references, you can talk to them as if you had grown up together.

One thing you don't ever want to do is offer to buy a drink for a strange girl. Generally, you are just wasting your money. One of my first rules of dating is: don't spend any money on the girl until you've established that she is friendly and possibly interested in you.

Besides, Shy Guys generally get this one wrong anyway. The usual Shy Guy way of buying someone a drink is this: you see a girl you like sitting across the bar. You call the bartender over. You tell the bartender the girl's next drink is on you. You pay for the drink without the girl knowing about it. Then you sneak out of the bar, telling the bartender not to reveal the identity of the mystery drink-buyer until you're gone.

There is a word for this approach: cowardly. It's also a big waste of money, because you're spending cash on someone who doesn't even know it was you! This is typical behavior for a Shy Guy—what I like to call the Half-assed Attempt.

All he's really done is confuse a girl who probably didn't even notice him sitting there in the first place. And even if she did notice him, she certainly wouldn't think very much of a man who is too frightened to talk to her. What kind of man is that?

There are a couple of other approaches I'd like to mention, one of which eliminates the need for a pickup line altogether. It involves seeing a pretty girl getting out of her car and then, once you are certain she is gone, leaving a business card or a note on her windshield with your name and phone number on it. This is a very cowardly approach, because the girl has no idea who left the note. She probably didn't notice you when she got out of her car. Probably 999 girls out of 1,000 would not call you in this situation. But there is that 1,000th girl, who just may be feeling a little curious and adventurous . . .

Another method is to bring a sketch pad or a notebook with you when you go to a coffee shop or a bar. Sit quietly by yourself, sketching or writing. There is always the possibility that some girl in the bar likes artistic types, and may come over to see what you're working on. If you do not have a creative side, you can simply bring a book to read, and hope some comely lass inquires about what you are reading.

So now you know which lines are the best and worst for a Shy Guy to use. But that's only step one. As any baseball player knows, the most important thing when you take a swing is to follow through. It's the same with pickup lines. The greatest pickup line in the world is useless if you haven't prepared a good follow-through.

Chapter Three

Closing the Deal

Closing the deal is the single most important thing for a Shy Guy to learn. Unfortunately, it's also the single most difficult thing, even harder than scaling the wall.

You see, any Shy Guy can reach the point where he is comfortable talking to girls. The difficult part comes in letting the girl know you are attracted to her and would like to go out with her. This is where most Shy Guys choke.

If you approach a girl in a bar, or in a park, or wherever, and make a couple of hours of conversation with her, and then you go your separate ways, making some empty promise that "Maybe I'll see you here again sometime!" you have really risked nothing. You haven't expressed a real interest in her. You haven't made any definite plans to see her again. You haven't made any kind of emotional connection. You're just going to be kicking yourself all the way home.

If you are serious about pursuing her, you have to let the girl know you're attracted to her and would like to see her again.

Usually Shy Guys like to convince themselves they'll have a second chance to ask out a girl. Well, it doesn't always work that way. You generally only get one chance.

You have to assume that the first time you meet a girl is your one and only shot with her. That after this, you are never going to see her again. So if you've got anything to say, you'd better say it then and there!

Believe me, you'll be much more satisfied going home with a sense of closure, knowing for better or for worse if you're ever going to see her again. There's nothing worse than not knowing. That leads to wasting too much time wondering, pondering what might happen, when you should be taking her out and having a good time, or pursuing other girls if you know she's not interested.

When you approach a girl for the first time, essentially you are selling yourself. You have to figure out what you can offer her that no other guy can. What are the qualities that make you unique. Are you smart? Are you funny? Do you have a lot of money? Are you a snappy dresser? Are you good at trivia? Any hidden talents? Do you have an unusual job? Can you offer her access to interesting people, big concerts, sporting events? Make the most of whatever connections you have. If there is something cool about you, don't keep it a secret—let her know about it!

Figure out the best qualities you have to offer and make sure you show them off. The best way to do that is to just be yourself. Let her get to know the real you. Find out what kind of things she is into, then steer the conversation in that direction. The main thing is that you be comfortable, so you come across as natural as possible.

If she starts talking about politics, and you know nothing about that topic, it may be time to change the subject. (As Calvin says in *Calvin and Hobbes*, "I know more about the private lives of celebrities than I do about government policy. I'm interested in things that are none of my business, and I'm bored by things that are important to know.") Try to steer the conversation toward topics that you are both knowledgeable about. If she winds up doing all the talking, she may think you either don't like her or that you have no personality. (Shy Guys are often accused of having no personality, when, in fact, they often have lots of personality, but only around people they feel comfortable with.)

You've got to use whatever talents you have to lure the girl in. If you can play guitar, pull it out and let her hear. If you are a good artist, draw a picture of her and let her see it.

When you first meet a new girl, you're like a salesman showing off a new car. And by agreeing to spend some time with you, the girl is basically taking a test drive. Sometimes it's a short drive, just down the street. Other times, it's a long, leisurely ride in the country. She really wants to see how you handle, what makes your engine run.

But after the drive is finished, it's up to you to close the deal. You've got to convince the girl that you are better than every other car on the lot. (As they say in *Hardbodies*, you've got to offer the girl a "BBD"—a "Bigger, Better Deal.")

As a Shy Guy, I don't like to ask a girl out unless I know for sure she is going to say yes. How do I know this? First I try to find out if she is single. If she has a boyfriend, you still have a chance, but it's a slim one. Most girls aren't going to cheat on their boyfriend for you. Although if a girl says she is having "problems" with her boyfriend, or that she is thinking of breaking up with him, you've got a much better shot. If she lives with her boyfriend, forget it; this is not even worth pursuing. It's still possible, but the cards are stacked against you. You're always better off going for a single girl—the odds are much better.

Always check for a wedding or engagement ring. You can save yourself hours of conversation by looking for that little band of gold on her left hand. You do not want to get involved with a married woman. I don't know about you, but I'm allergic to lead poisoning, if you get my meaning.

You've established that the girl is single. What next? During the course of the conversation, see if she talks about things you and she can do together in the future. Often, girls will say things like, "That movie looks good! We should go see it!" Or, "Racketball looks like a lot of fun! Will you show me how to play it sometime?" Or, "We should go to that club together!"

These are just little clues a girl gives you to tell you there is hope for the future. One thing I like to do before I ask out any girl is to determine if she and I are really compatible. Are we *really* hitting it off? Does she seem genuinely interested in getting to know me, and wanting to spend more time with me in the future? Or is she just making friendly conversation? Just because a girl acts polite doesn't necessarily mean she is interested in dating you. What I try to do is determine if we are actually "clicking." Are we really a good match for each other? Do we have anything in common, besides a physical attraction and a desire to not be alone?

In the best scenario, there is strong mutual interest. If you spend hours talking together, and the time flies by, and you can't wait to see her again when the night is over, this is a good girl to date. If there are a lot of awkward silences and you are straining to come up with things to say, the two of you are not hitting it off, no matter how much you both may wish it otherwise. If you are really connecting with someone, the conversation will never stop flowing.

If I meet a new girl, and we are struggling for conversation, I sometimes like to give her the benefit of the doubt. Maybe she is just shy and she will show more of her personality once she gets to know me better. Generally, though, if two people don't hit it off the first night, odds are they never will.

Once you've determined whether the two of you are really

interested in each other, try to assess what her schedule is like. Does she go to school full time and work nights? This girl may be too busy for any guy at this time. Is her schedule compatible with yours? Is she geographically desirable? (In other words, does she live as close or as far as you want her to be?) No point in wasting time on someone you can never see.

Once you've determined that a girl is definitely single, has some free time, is geographically desirable, and is attracted to you (another good clue here is if she actually tells you how attractive she finds you—it happens sometimes!), then it's time for you to move in for the kill.

The most important thing to do when you meet a girl who likes you is to get the seven digits. There is a great satisfaction that comes from closing a deal. You have put yourself on sale, made the best pitch you could possibly make, and found an interested buyer. To a Shy Guy, that is the ultimate accomplishment.

Now you're ready for that first date, to see if she wants to test-drive you all the way home. (Sorry, I got a little carried away with the new car analogy!)

Before you can close any deals, though, you're going to have to learn some important lessons about

What Girls Say...And What They Really Mean

You have to realize that the dating game has rules just like any other game. It helps if you know the rules of the game before you play. One important thing to know is that most girls are too polite to ever give you a flat-out rejection. Over the years, women have developed subtle ways of rejecting men that don't involve doing it face-to-face.

Generally, most girls like to leave you smiling, keeping alive the hope of seeing them again in the future—even if the girl really never wants to see you again. The thinking here is that an empty promise will give you a few nights of happiness, whereas a quick rejection will only bring instant unhappiness and hurt feelings. Most girls prefer to give guys a glimmer of hope, as false as that hope may be.

Unfortunately, most Shy Guys tend to be hopeless romantics, and they keep hoping that glimmer will develop into a bright glow. In order to save the Shy Guys of the world future heartache, I've compiled this list of tactful things girls say when they are rejecting you, though you may not know it at the time.

What a Girl Says . . .	***What She Means . . .***
1) I'm just going to the ladies' room. I'll be right back.	I have no interest in you. I'm not coming back from the ladies' room.
2) I promise I'll be right back! I swear I will!	She's definitely not coming back. The more she insists she will be "right back" from the ladies' room, the greater the odds you will never see her again.
3) I like you as a friend.	I have no interest in you sexually.
4) I'll meet you at the club.	I'm not going to the club. (Girls never meet any guy anywhere. They either go with you, or they're not going.)

5) I come here all the time. I'll see you the next time you're here.	I never come here. I've never been here before, and I'll certainly never come back again!
6) I never give out my number. Why don't you give me *your* number instead?	I don't want you to have my phone number. I'm never going to call you!
7) I'll give you my work number.	I don't want you to have my home number.
8) That guy is just a friend.	I'm sleeping with that guy.
9) I'm really good friends with the band.	I'm having sex with some guys in the band.
10) I'm not sure when I can see you again, because I'm really busy.	I'm not that busy, I just don't ever want to see you again!
11) I really don't want to date anyone right now.	I'll date anyone! I just don't want to date you!
12) I'll call you right back!	Don't hold your breath!
13) I've got your number!	I threw away your number!
14) I'm not allowed to date customers.	You frighten me!

Now you know some quick, easy ways to tell if you are being rejected. It is important to be aware that a girl is blowing you off; this is an area where Shy Guys tend to be a little naive. Being aware of the little warning signs of rejection can help your love life, and save you a lot of wasted time.

Sometimes you meet a girl and spend the next month trying to arrange a date with her. It may be that the girl really does like you, but just isn't willing to make the time for you. If this is the case, you may want to give up on this girl and move on to someone else.

I usually find that if you get a girl's phone number and spend two weeks trying to set up a date with her with no luck, it's never going to happen. After that two-week grace period, the girl starts to forget what you even look like, and why she was even interested in you in the first place. At this point, it's best to cut your losses and throw her number away. If she had really wanted to go out with you, she would have done so.

As I've noted before, this stuff is supposed to be fun, not work. Arranging a date should be a simple yes or no proposition. Either she wants to go out with you or she doesn't. If she keeps giving you the runaround, it's a subtle way of saying, "I'm really not interested."

One thing I should mention here is that just because you have gotten a girl's phone number and she has agreed to go out with you doesn't mean it's a done deal. Many times a girl will cancel at the last minute. Often a girl will agree to go out with you, only to change her mind. Maybe the night she met you she thought you were a great catch, but the next day she woke up and said, "What was I thinking?"

Planning a date and going out on a date can be two entirely different things. I've had girls who actually picked what movie they wanted to see with me, and what time, and what restaurant we were going to eat at only to bail out at the last minute. It happens. Just as you may decide that a girl you've met is not exactly your type, so, too, girls may decide you're not what they're looking for after all. I like to say it's not officially a date until you ring her doorbell and she's standing there, dressed and ready.

A good rule of thumb is not to tell anyone about your date until after it actually happens. If you tell everyone about it beforehand, and it winds up not happening, you feel like a chump.

It's also a good idea to have a back-up plan ready in case your date blows you off, so you're not left high and dry. What I often do is make arrangements to go out with my friends, while secretly planning to go out with a girl. This way, if the girl has a last minute change of heart, I just go out with my friends, acting as if that is what I had intended to do all along. If the girl does come through, I simply tell my friends there has been a change in plans.

One other thing I want to warn you about is not to attempt the Spontaneous Date. If you call a girl on Friday afternoon and ask her out for Friday night, 99 percent of the time, she will say no. Even if she has no plans for that night, no one wants to seem like they have nothing to do on a Friday night.

This can be frustrating for a Shy Guy, who is used to calling his boyhood friends up at a moment's notice and arranging a spontaneous night out. It just doesn't work that way with girls. Unless you have tickets to see Pearl Jam, my advice is to never attempt to ask a girl out for a same-day date. You always have to give girls at least one day's notice, preferably more.

Okay, we've covered the dark side of dating, now let's look at the good news. Just as you can usually figure out you are being rejected (the fact that she went to the bathroom two hours ago and never came back is usually a good indication), so, too, can you often pick up subtle hints that a girl really likes you. Consider the following list:

TOP TEN WAYS TO TELL IF A GIRL LIKES YOU

1) She gives you her undivided attention.
2) She blows off her friends for you.
3) She returns your phone calls as soon as she receives

your messages or she calls you back the instant you beep her.

4) She talks about things the two of you will do in the future.
5) She is willing to change her plans for you.
6) She goes out of her way to do something nice for you, like bake you cookies or buy you a present.
7) When you go out on dates, she insists on paying for stuff on an equal basis (i.e., you pay this time, she pays next time). However, if she pays for her own stuff every time, that means she probably isn't interested in you sexually, doesn't want to lead you on, and doesn't want to feel indebted to you in any way.
8) She shows a strong interest in your life, asking a lot of questions about your hobbies, family, job, etc.
9) She changes something about her appearance just because she knows it will make you happy (for instance, she gets a new haircut, starts wearing shorter skirts, shaves her armpit hair).
10) She offers you a sip of her drink, or takes a sip out of yours (Essentially she's telling you she's willing to swap saliva with you!).
11) She is willing to break her stride for you (In other words, when she is walking down the street and she sees you coming toward her, she stops in her tracks and talks to you. If a girl does not like you, she will keep right on walking. She may give you a friendly hello, but she will never break her stride).
12) After you open the car door and let her into your car, she reaches over and unlocks your door for you. This was demonstrated in the 1993 Robert De Niro movie, *A Bronx Tale*, but it was something I had been aware of for years. Girls who fail to unlock the door for you

tend to be vain and self-absorbed. Girls who go out of their way to unlock the door for you tend to be very thoughtful and considerate of other people.

Of course, these days, thanks to the miracles of modern technology, the driver of the car can automatically unlock both doors from twenty feet away, so it's becoming more and more of a moot point. In fact, thanks to keyless entry, it is no longer necessary for a guy to walk around to the passenger side of the car and unlock the door for the girl. Any guy who does it these days is doing it out of a true sense of chivalry and gallantry. This may be something for you guys to consider doing if you're looking to score some points!

Even though we live in enlightened times, in which girls like to be treated as equals, there are still quite a few females out there who like to be given the royal treatment. You know, open their car door, pull out their chair, the whole nine yards. Personally, I draw the line at putting my coat over a mud puddle so she doesn't get her shoes dirty. Your own level of chivalry may vary.

And then of course, there's this sure-fire method of telling if a girl likes you . . .

She lets you have sex with her!

(That's when you can tell she really, *really* likes you. Either that, or she's really easy!)

As far as how to tell if you really like a girl, I've got one sure-fire answer: you're willing to spend money on her. It's that simple. For instance, let's say you ask out a girl, and she says she wants to go out to an expensive restaurant for dinner. If you like the girl, you will say yes in a heartbeat. You would spend any amount of money on her, do anything for her. (Shy Guys tend to be pretty extreme in their feelings.)

It doesn't matter whether you actually have the money or not. I know guys who've been unemployed, bankrupt, and heavily in debt, but they would still whip out that credit card in a heartbeat if it meant impressing a pretty girl. As long as you have a credit card, you're never really out of money!

But if you're not sure how you really feel about her, you may balk at spending a lot of money on her. You may suggest a cheaper restaurant, or a movie instead. (Offer to pick her up at nine, to ensure that she will have already eaten dinner by the time you get there!)

That is my ultimate deciding factor to determine if a girl really is the one for you. If you are ga-ga over her, the sky's the limit. If you have any doubts, though, you may suggest to her that you go Dutch! There's no better indicator than your wallet to show the value you place on a relationship.

Of course, there are more romantic ways to tell if you really like a girl. One is that you think about her all the time. Everything you see, every song you hear on the radio, reminds you of her. If you walk down the street and every girl you see on the street looks like her, then, my friend, you have been bitten by the love bug!

Don't Be a Stalker!

The one thing I can't stress enough to my fellow Shy Guys is the importance of persistence when it comes to dating. You can't just ask a girl out once and then give up. You've got to keep asking her until she says yes.

There are a million reasons a girl might turn you down when you first ask her for a date, some of which have nothing to do with you. Maybe you caught her at a bad time. Maybe she's going through a messy breakup. Maybe she just happens to be legitimately busy. That's why it's often worth your while to hang in there.

Just remember that there is a fine line between persistence and desperation. If you pursue her too aggressively, you may wind up scaring her away. It's important that the girl think of you as a normal guy and not some deranged stalker.

One thing Shy Guys tend to have in common with stalkers is intensity of focus. If there is something a Shy Guy wants, he can obsess about it, lose sleep over it, let it consume his life—especially if the thing in question happens to be a girl. The same is true for stalkers, who also have a tendency to obsess about women they desire.

So how do you know when you've crossed that fine line between being a persistent nice guy and an aggressive stalker? Here are a few pointers:

A persistent guy . . . calls a girl several times in an effort to make a date.
A stalker . . . leaves a hundred messages a day, with the messages gradually getting more threatening as the day goes on!

A persistent guy . . . arranges an "accidental" meeting where he can bump into the object of his affections.
A stalker . . . hides in the bushes outside her house, waiting to jump out and surprise her when she comes home!

A persistent guy . . . sends her a love letter, expressing his true feelings.
A stalker . . . cuts out words and letters from magazines, just in case he needs to compose a ransom note!

A persistent guy . . . asks a girl's friends about her likes and dislikes.
A stalker . . . hires a private detective to follow her around and really dig up some dirt on her!

A persistent guy . . . keeps a picture of her in his wallet, for inspiration.
A stalker . . . builds a shrine to her in his bedroom, consisting of thousands of photos and candles, and prays before it every night!

A persistent guy . . . is not deterred by an initial rejection.
A stalker . . . is not deterred by a restraining order!

A persistent guy . . . refers to his intended girl as "potential girlfriend material."
A stalker . . . refers to his intended as "my fiancée," "my soulmate," or my "immortal beloved"!

A persistent guy . . . wants a girl to think of him as someone who works hard to get what he wants.
A stalker . . . wants a girl to think of him as someone who could get violent if he doesn't get his way!

A persistent guy . . . eventually knows when to give up if she's not interested.
A stalker . . . knows that just because you're in prison, it doesn't mean you have to stop pursuing her!

A persistent guy . . . watches romantic movies for inspiration.
A stalker . . . watches *Fatal Attraction* and roots for the stalker!

A persistent guy . . . says, "Oh well—she has a boyfriend. I guess I don't have a chance."
A stalker . . . says, "Sure, she's got a boyfriend today. But there's all kinds of accidents that could happen."

A persistent guy . . . sends her flowers and candy to prove his affections.
A stalker . . . kidnaps her favorite pet and sends it back to her, piece by piece!

A persistent guy . . . reads women's magazines to pick up tips on how to woo her.
A stalker . . . subscribes to military magazines to keep up with all the latest high-tech surveillance technology!

A persistent guy . . . remembers little things about her, like her favorite color, her favorite food, and her favorite vacation spot.
A stalker . . . has her entire schedule memorized, from the time she wakes up to the time she goes to sleep!

A persistent guy . . . buys himself a snappy new suit to catch her eye.
A stalker . . . buys a camoflage suit so she won't see him prowling around outside her house!

A persistent guy . . . stocks up on breath mints, cologne, and romantic CDs.
A stalker . . . buys ropes, handcuffs, and other items used to keep guests around for a while!

A persistent guy . . . drops in at her office unexpectedly to invite her to lunch.

A stalker . . . gets a job in the same building, just to keep an eye on her!

A persistent guy . . . knows when to admit defeat. He says, "Well, I gave it my best shot. I guess it just wasn't meant to be."
A stalker . . . never gives up! He says, "If I can't have her, no one can!"

So there you have it! Now you know the difference between a stalker and a persistent guy. Study those differences, and try to remember them. This way, you'll never find a pesky thing like a court order getting in the way of your pursuit of your ideal girl.

Anatomy of a Pickup

So far, I've discussed my suggestions for the best and worst opening lines, and you've heard my theories about closing the deal. A lot of my suggestions involve planning out everything in advance, knowing what to say and when to say it, how to tell if a girl is interested in you, and how to know when to either bail out or finish what what you started.

All of these ideas may sound good to you in theory, but you may be wondering how they work in practice. After all, you have to be quick on your feet, be able to switch strategies on a moment's notice, and know which approach is best for which situation.

All right then—come with me now as I walk you through a typical meeting between a Shy Guy and a girl at a party. I'm only going to do this once, so pay attention.

It starts out with the Shy Guy scanning the room, finding the one girl he is most interested in, ensuring that she is, in fact, single, and then positioning himself next to her. He may or may not choose to establish eye contact with her first. I don't think it's necessary, but many other experts in the field would disagree with me. We'll leave that one to your discretion.

Of course, after the conversation has actually started, eye contact is essential. Lock onto her eyes and do not turn away. Do not look at her breasts. Focus on her eyes. If another girl walks by that you find attractive, *do not* look at her. You will only blow your chance. When you are talking to a girl, she should be the only girl who exists for you at that moment.

Keep your hands away from your face. Shy Guys have a tendency to cover up their mouths when they talk. Speak clearly—don't slur. Open your mouth. And for God's sake, don't talk with your mouth full!

After positioning himself with conversational distance, the Shy Guy taps her on the shoulder. (It's always a good idea to rap a girl on the shoulder when you first meet her, because it clearly establishes that she is the one you are talking to. Most girls don't expect a total stranger to suddenly start talking to them, so a friendly tap helps clarify things.)

Their conversation goes like this:

SHY GUY: Excuse me, is your name Kelly?

(The Guy has opened with the Mistaken Identity Ploy. A classic Shy Guy line. One of the very best lines for beginners to start with.)

GIRL: No, it's Lisa.

SHY GUY: I'm sorry. It's just that you look just like this girl I went to college with. Did you go to City College?

GIRL: Actually, I do go to City College now!

(A happy coincidence! The Mistaken Identity Ploy worked like a charm! Now the Shy Guy's claim of knowing the girl seems to have some validity.)

SHY GUY: That's probably where I know you from. When did you start there?

GIRL: This is my second year.

(The Shy Guy has just determined the girl's age, assuming she went straight to college after high school. Another good way to do this is to ask her what year she finished high school.)

SHY GUY: Oh. I finished City College in '94, so I was gone by the time you got there. When I was there, they used to have a bar off-campus called Chuck's. It was pretty wild.

(Note that the Shy Guy has now completely abandoned the Mistaken Identity Ploy at this point, and has segued into a conversation about campus life. By mentioning a popular campus hangout, the Shy Guy has introduced an element of familiarity to the conversation. This potentially establishes a bond between the two of them.)

GIRL: I love that place! The last time I was there, I got so wasted!

(So far, so good. The bond is holding. Now it's up to the Shy Guy to take the ball and run with it. He's going to have to tell some more stories about himself. This is the primary way people make conversation. If you are not comfortable talking about yourself, you will never get over your shyness.)

SHY GUY: I had so many great times there. One night, Pearl Jam played on campus, and afterward, a couple of guys from the band came in and hung out at the bar! Those guys are great!

(It has been said there are three levels of conversation: Fact, Opinion, and Philosophy. Here, the Shy Guy has moved from level one to level two.)

GIRL: Yeah. I saw them once at Madison Square Garden.

(The girl has just offered some information which the guy did not ask for. This shows that she is potentially interested.)

SHY GUY: That must've been a good show.

(The Shy Guy has phrased his question in the form of a statement.

This is a good way to avoid asking too many questions when you first meet someone.)

GIRL: It was pretty good. But after the show, we missed the train home, and I had to sleep in the train station!

(By telling a little story about herself, the girl has opened up a little bit to the Shy Guy. In essence, she's telling him, "I want to get to know you better. Let's talk.")

SHY GUY: That's funny—I saw them at the Meadowlands, and not only did my car get broken into, but my friend got arrested!

(The Shy Guy has just begun his own story. It is important to watch the expression on the girl's face here. Is she listening to the story, or does she only want to talk about herself?)

GIRL: What happened?

(Good—she asked a question. She's interested. Proceed with the story.)

SHY GUY: He got a little drunk and started mouthing off to a cop. I don't go to too many concerts any more. Mostly I go to the local rock clubs, like the Hard Rock and the Pit Stop.

(One of my first rules is to establish where she lives. By mentioning local hangouts, you can establish where she is from and if she is geographically desirable.)

GIRL: I've been to both of those. I live right around the corner from the Hard Rock!

(The Shy Guy has gotten an answer to his question without actually asking his question. That's good.)

SHY GUY: I live right here in town, too! My name is Joe.

GIRL: Nice to meet you.

(There really is no easy way to introduce yourself, so you may as well do it as early in the conversation as possible. If the girl offers to shake your hand here, and gives you an extended handshake, that's a good sign. Unsolicited physical contact. Also, pay attention to how often she touches you during the conversation. Does she grab your arm to make a point? Does she get unnecessarily

close, or put an arm on your shoulder? Any physical contact may imply that she wants to get intimate with you. Or she may just be a very physical person, so pay attention. Does she touch every person she talks to, or just you?)

GIRL: Last week, I saw this local band, the Headspins, at the Hard Rock. It was a great show. They played till four in the morning!

(It's going well—she's offering lots of unsolicited information. Full steam ahead.)

SHY GUY: There are are lots of good rock clubs in this area. Do you ever go to Rock Candy?

GIRL: No, I hardly ever go out anymore.

(Warning! Warning! Danger, Will Robinson! She hardly ever goes out? That's a clear indication that she may have a boyfriend! Proceed with caution!)

SHY GUY: Why is that?

GIRL: I work a lot of nights, and I'm in school, so that doesn't leave a lot of time for partying.

(Excellent! She didn't mention a boyfriend. That doesn't necessarily mean she's single, though. You must use cunning to get that information.)

SHY GUY: What are you studying?

GIRL: I'm learning to be a gourmet cook.

SHY GUY: I bet your boyfriend must be happy about that!

(The Shy Guy has just cleverly asked the girl if she has a boyfriend, again, without directly asking her the question.)

GIRL: I don't have a boyfriend.

SHY GUY: A beautiful girl like you? I can't believe it!

(The Shy Guy has just expressed his interest in the girl by telling her that essentially he finds her attractive and considers her to be a good catch.)

GIRL: I was seeing someone, but we broke up a few months ago.

(Perfect! Clear the runway! We're primed for takeoff! It's important to establish if she has a serious boyfriend as early in the conversation as possible. If she does have one, there's really no point in continuing, now is there?)

SHY GUY: Where do you work?

(The Shy Guy has quickly changed the subject. He doesn't want to hear about her ex-boyfriend.)

GIRL: I'm a waitress at Martoni's Restaurant.

SHY GUY: I've heard they have the best pizza in town.

(Again, the question in the form of a statement.)

GIRL: It's really good. You should come in sometime.

(Bingo! She's definitely interested! She just asked the Shy Guy to come visit her at work! That's a good sign.)

SHY GUY: I'll have to do that. What nights do you work?

GIRL: Thursday, Friday, and Saturday nights. Where do you work?

(This is good—now she's asking questions about you. This implies a strong interest.)

SHY GUY: I'm a lion tamer.

GIRL: A lion tamer?

SHY GUY: Well, somebody's got to do it!

(This is a crucial juncture. The Shy Guy has just made a little joke. How the girl reacts to the joke will determine if their personalities are compatible or not.)

GIRL: What a coincidence! It happens I've got a wild lion at home, and I need to domesticate him.

SHY GUY: Bring him in. We'll put him up on the lift and see what's wrong with him!

(Great! She played along with the joke! She may be compatible with him! Proceed.)

GIRL: So what do you do when you're not taming lions?

SHY GUY: Well, I work for a publishing company.

GIRL: Really? What type of things do you publish?
(All right! She's interested in his career! That's a great sign!)

SHY GUY: We only publish books about David Hasselhoff. You know, the guy from *Baywatch.*
(Again, the Shy Guy makes with the jokes. You want a girl with a good sense of humor.)

GIRL: I can see where there'd be a lot of demand for that. Actually, you even look a little like David Hasselhoff!

SHY GUY: Is that good or bad?

GIRL: That's good! I think he's very handsome!
(Excellent! In a roundabout way, the girl has just told the Shy Guy she finds him attractive!)

SHY GUY: Well, I do have one thing in common with him. He's a rock star in Germany, and I like to play guitar.

GIRL: I've always wanted to learn how to play guitar!
(She's hooked! Now he just has to reel her in!)

SHY GUY: It's not that hard, really.

GIRL: Will you teach me?

SHY GUY: Sure.

GIRL: That would be great!
(The Shy Guy has Hand in this situation [as they say on Seinfeld*], because now the girl is depending on him to help her with something.)*

GIRL: So what else do you do for fun?

SHY GUY: Well, I like to shoot pool with my friends.

GIRL: I love pool! We'll have to play sometime!
(All right! They've got something in common! This is going rather well! The fact that she is talking about the future is also a good sign. That shows she has plans for him beyond this one conversation.)

SHY GUY: What kind of music do you listen to?

GIRL: I like alternative. I listen to just about everything except rap and country.
(Excellent! Sounds like this girl is exactly his type!)

SHY GUY: Me, too.

GIRL: And I love classical music!
(Ugh! Oh well! You can't expect to have everything in common!)

GIRL: So do you live at home, or . . . ?

SHY GUY: I have roommates.
(This is a good line of questioning. She wants to know what your social situation is. Are you some kind of mama's boy, sponging off your parents, or are you independent? Girls like independent.)

SHY GUY: How about you?

GIRL: I live with roommates.
(Cool! If she lives with her parents, that decreases your odds of scoring. If she has roommates, that gives her a lot more freedom to come and go as she pleases.)

GIRL: Do you have a girlfriend?
(Great! She asked the big question! It's okay for girls to ask this of guys. Shy Guys almost never ask a girl if she has a boyfriend, but girls have no problem asking guys.)

SHY GUY: No. I recently ended a relationship, too.
(Say this even if you are lying. It's important to establish to the girl that you are capable of normal, healthy relationships with the opposite sex. It beats saying, "I haven't had a girlfriend in five years. Mostly I hang out in go-go bars, then I masturbate myself to sleep every night!")

GIRL: Who are you here with?

SHY GUY: A couple of friends. That's them over there.
(Girls will always ask who you are with. This is their subtle way of finding out if you have a girlfriend. Also, they want to find out if you have any cute friends they can hook up with their girlfriends.)

SHY GUY: Actually, we almost didn't make it here tonight. We were going to go to the new Schwarzenegger movie instead.

GIRL: I saw that movie! It's great! You have to see it!

SHY GUY: I'd like to. I just don't have anyone to see it with.

(The Shy Guy has just asked out the girl, without actually asking her out. You see, if you never actually ask the girl out, she can't actually reject you!)

GIRL: I'll see it with you! I want to see it again!

(Put a fork in her! She's done!)

SHY GUY: Okay! What night is good for you? I guess you can't really go out on weekends . . .

GIRL: Oh, I can take off work easily. Just pick a night.

(Whoa! She's willing to rearrange her schedule for him! This girl is smitten! Time for the Shy Guy to bring it home.)

SHY GUY: How's Friday night?

GIRL: That's fine. As long as I tell my manager a day in advance, it's no problem.

(Time to close the deal!)

SHY GUY: Let me get your number.

(At this point, the girl writes down her phone number for the Shy Guy.)

GIRL: Here's my home number . . . and here's my beeper number.

(Her beeper number, too? Boy, this girl really likes this guy! I'm surprised she didn't give him her work number, too!)

GIRL: And here's my work number!

(What did I tell you! She's crazy for him!)

SHY GUY: Well, I should be getting back to my friends.

(Sometimes if you walk away from a girl before the night is over, it makes you look cooler—like you're not that desperate. This makes her think that you are a loyal, supportive friend, and not just some guy who came out looking to score. Of course, if you

and the girl are really hitting it off, by all means abandon your friends and devote all your attention to her.)

GIRL: Me and my friends are going to the diner later. You guys should meet us there.

(Whoa! She suggested the change of scenery! There's no question that this girl is most definitely interested! If she were any more interested, they'd be shopping for an engagement ring!)

SHY GUY: I'm not sure what my friends want to do later, but maybe we'll see you there! It was nice meeting you.

GIRL: Nice meeting you, too!

(Notice how the Shy Guy did not give the girl a definite answer about meeting her later. He was smart. He played it cool. If you seem too eager, you often blow your chances. Your best bet is to give her a vague promise that you might be there, but don't guarantee anything. You want to keep her guessing—keep an air of mystery about whether you really like her or not. When two people meet in a bar or at a party, there are often a lot of broken promises. Girls tend to not expect anything from these kind of meetings. In this way, she will be pleasantly surprised if you do show up later, and you will be a much better catch in her eyes.)

Chapter Four

The Best Places to Meet Girls

Where can I go to meet girls? This is a question commonly asked by Shy Guys.

In this book, I talk a lot about bars, because that is the place where guys and gals most often go to meet each other. But a lot of Shy Guys are not comfortable meeting chicks in bars. What to do about them?

According to a survey published in *USA Today*, the most popular place for ladies and gents to meet is at parties. Well, Shy Guys don't get invited to a lot of parties, and they tend to not feel comfortable there even if they do receive that rare invitation. Usually if a Shy Guy goes to a party, he brings along a couple of other Shy Guys and they huddle together in a corner all night.

"Mingling" is not a Shy Guy's strong suit.

Other common ways to meet girls are through friends and at the workplace. Well, what if there are no girls in your social circle? And what if there are no women in your workplace, or none you're attracted to?

Have no fear, Shy Guys of the world. I've got some suggestions for you.

First of all, I'd recommend bars over clubs. Girls who go to clubs seem to go just to dance and hang out with their friends. Plus, the music is so loud in these places, it can make conversation difficult. With bars, the focus is more on conversation, playing darts and pool, and watching sports on TV. Bars are far more conducive to conversation.

If you do go to a disco, I strongly recommend trying to meet a girl while you are waiting in line outside the club. This may be the one chance you really have to talk to her in a quiet setting. Plus, if you meet her before you get inside the club, you will have a connection with her. She will trust you more than any guy she meets inside.

Another problem with dance clubs is that they tend to be too crowded. You might think that the more people that are in one place, the better your chances of picking up. I usually find that the opposite is true: The larger the crowd in a nightclub, the worse your chances are. It generally means you only have more competition. Your best bet is to go out on weeknights, when the clubs are not as crowded. You are far more likely to meet someone on a slow night, when things are a little quieter, and the girl has far less distractions.

One of the best places to meet girls, believe it or not, is in a country-western saloon. These places are usually filled with girls who love to dance. You're not into Garth Brooks? No problem! Nobody hates country music more than I do, but I must say I've had a fair amount of success picking up some little fillies at the local country-western bar.

Girls at country-western bars tend to be very friendly. If you're in a two-steppin' mood, you can show up early and take line-dancing lessons. Then, when the night begins, you'll be ready to do the Boot-Scootin' Boogie all night long! I find the girls you meet in a country bar tend to be very old-fashioned and wholesome; their idea of a good time is to go out and dance the night away. These are the types of girls you want to meet.

Even if you don't like the idea of dancing in line all night, jumping around and shaking your fanny like some mixed-up little Macarena monkey, a country-western bar can still be fun. You can just go and shoot pool and watch all the babes dance. Sit by the bar and when a cowgirl you like comes your way, well, you just lasso that little lady and mosey on back to your ranch.

One of my favorite places to meet girls is the beach. I like it because you don't have all the distractions of a bar—huge crowds, loud music, etc. It is a place where you can actually have a quiet conversation with someone. It is also one of the few places a girl will go alone.

As a Shy Guy, I don't like having other people listening in when I'm putting the moves on someone. It's uncomfortable enough talking to a new girl for the first time—the last thing I want is an audience. If a girl is with her friends, it only increases the odds of your being laughed at when you walk away. If a girl is alone, at least she'll keep her laughter to herself.

A successful pick-up should be like a good bank heist—a quick in and out, nobody gets hurt, no witnesses, and everybody involved keeps their mouths shut. You don't want any nosy cops coming around asking questions later. The most important thing about planning a good heist is that you . . . oh, er, ahem. I got a little sidetracked there. Sorry. Where was I? Oh, yes—the beach.

There are many different ways to approach a girl on the beach. If she has just been swimming in the ocean, ask her how the water is. If she is sitting nearby, ask her to watch your stuff while you go get a soda. (This will establish a bond between the two of you that can come in handy when you get back.) You may even offer to buy her a soda or a bottled water, as well, since she is being nice enough to watch your stuff.

Another place where girls often go by themselves is the mall. Sometimes you will see them sitting on a bench, taking a break from shopping. All you have to do is join them. Other times, you can position yourself on a bench, and wait till a pretty girl comes and sits next to you.

One good thing to do at the mall is find a store that interests you, and approach girls who shop there. Occasionally you may find it necessary to follow a cute girl into a store you really have no interest in. In this case, you may have to do some fast talking to explain your presence in the store.

If you see a girl shopping in a men's clothing store, she may be shopping for a present for her father, her brother, or her boyfriend. (Or maybe she just likes to wear men's clothes! You see that kind of thing a lot these days!) Find out which is the case before pursuing her any further.

You may be inclined to follow a young lass into a ladies' clothing store. In this instance, explain to the girl that you are shopping for a birthday present for your sister, and ask her what types of things would make good gifts. Whenever possible, try to assume the role of Clueless Boy.

A rock concert is a great place to meet a girl. Maybe you can even meet someone while you are in line at Ticketmaster, purchasing your concert tickets. Ask her what artist she is buying tickets for. Maybe the two of you are going to the same concert. If so, you know right off the bat that you have something in common. If things work out, maybe you can even go to the concert together.

If you live in a small town, you may want to take a little walk through the center of town in the middle of the afternoon. You will often see pretty girls walking alone, shopping. The approach

I like to use here is to ask the girl where I can find the nearest ATM machine, or the location of the post office. (Hey, there goes Retarded Boy again! Lives in a town for twenty years and doesn't even know where the post office is!)

This method is not as effective if you live in a big city. I consider the ultimate challenge for a pickup artist to be meeting a girl on the mean streets of New York City. My basic feeling is that girls growing up in the Big City are very suspicious, paranoid, and highly distrustful of strangers. They have spent their whole lives avoiding conversations with strange men on the streets. You've got to overcome a lifetime of ingrained big city behavior.

If you can pull this one off you're a better man than I. (Jerry Seinfeld meets girls on the streets of New York all the time on TV, but this is real life we're talking about here.) Even though I worked in Manhattan for four years, I was always afraid I was going to get Maced, so I never even attempted it. If you are brave enough to attempt the City Streets Pickup, I'd recommend waiting until the girl enters a restaurant or store, and talk to her there instead. A store provides a more comfortable atmosphere, since one of you can always leave the store if it's not going well. Indoors, surrounded by other people, most women feel less vulnerable and are more open to meeting guys.

One place you may not have tried yet is the car wash. Go to one of those places where the customers get out of their cars while the car wash crew cleans their vehicle. Hand over your car keys and go sit with the other patrons. If one of the other consumers is a cute girl, you can chat her up! Ask her about her car; tell her about yours. See where it goes from there.

If you ever see a girl with a "For Sale" sign in the window of her car; by all means, use this as an excuse to talk to her, even if you have absolutely no interest in actually buying the car. For that matter, if you see a girl with an apartment for rent, pay her a visit, and ask lots of questions. This also applies if you see a cute salesgirl working somewhere (anywhere). I think it's perfectly legitimate to pose as a potential customer if it will further your social life. For instance, if you know a girl who is a travel agent, you can fake an interest in traveling to some exotic location. Go to her office and ask her lots of questions. Pretend to be interested, up to a point, but don't tease her too long. At some point, make it clear that you'd like to take her out.

In *Fast Times at Ridgemont High*, Rat has a crush on a girl who works at the Fotomat and spends the summer buying forty dollars' worth of film from her—but he never gets around to asking the girl out. Shy Guys often get themselves into this situation. They spend lots of money at a place, intending to get to know the salesgirl, but wind up never actually talking to her. You really want to close the deal before you go broke.

What about the video store? Surely that must be a great place to pick up, right? I'm not so sure. Whenever you see a girl in a video store, there is always the possibility she is renting a movie that she can go home and watch with her boyfriend. In fact, often, when a couple enters a video store together, the guy will head toward the action section and the girl will head toward the chick flicks, then they will come together to make a decision. So if you see a girl you like in the video store, keep an eye on her for a minute or two to see who she's with. There is nothing more embarrassing than when you are putting the moves on some girl and her boyfriend walks over and puts his arm around her. A good rule of thumb is this: Always assume a girl has a boyfriend unless you see evidence that proves otherwise. If you detect no indication of a boyfriend, walk right up next to her as she scans the wall of videos and say, "That's a great movie!" or "Have you seen that one?"

If you're the religious sort, you may want to treat your church as a sort of holy singles bar. You can meet lots of wholesome, old-fashioned girls in church. Many churches sponsor activities that offer good people-meeting opportunities. Festivals and fairs are also great bets.

Other good places to meet girls: the library (just do it quietly), a CD store, a pet store, or any other place that sells things you're interested in. And if you live in the South, you may want to go cruising at a family reunion. (Just kidding!)

The main idea is to do things that interest you, and try to find a girl who enjoys doing the same things. One of my favorite activities is to go to a local bar and shoot pool with my friends. After we've played a few games, we'll ask some girls at the bar to join us in a game. This way, we're having a good time, doing something we enjoy, and if we happen to meet some girls, even better!

You may want to try Rollerblading. It is an incredibly popular activity right now—especially among girls. It provides good aerobic exercise, and it gets you outside for an hour or two. Why not find a local park or beach that has a Rollerblading or biking path and give it a shot? After you finish blading, you can find a quiet spot to sit down and talk with some girls. Maybe you'll meet a girl who is also Rollerblading and you'll already have something in common. (You can ask her how many miles she is doing today, or where she got her equipment.) You may even want to ask her to blade alongside you.

I should add here that the pursuit of a lifemate can be an intensely frustrating one. Sometimes you will go for months without results.

If you focus all your energy on getting a girlfriend and end up with one rejection after another, the pursuit stops being fun, and becomes depressing. There's nothing worse than putting all your time and energy into something and getting absolutely nothing in return.

If you're getting shot down every time you open your mouth,

chasing girls can be the most frustrating thing in the world. How many ego blows can one human being stand? Every time you approach a new girl, you are presenting yourself to her, body and soul, and if she blows you off, she's not just rejecting your pickup line—it feels as if she's rejecting you as a human being. That can only happen to you so many times in one lifetime before it starts to get to you.

And yet, the only solution is to keep on trying. That's why I recommend making it as much fun as possible. Go out with your friends to have a good time; bust a move on every girl who seems approachable and fun, and if something happens, great. If not, don't worry about it. It will happen eventually.

Unfortunately, as Tom Petty notes, the waiting is the hardest part. You know that, eventually, you're going to meet a nice girl and settle down, but it's easy to lose your faith in the meantime. All I can do is encourage you to be patient. You made it through puberty, which is the most difficult time of all to be shy. Surely you can wait a little while longer.

Now, this brings us to kind of a gray area: What about waitresses, salesgirls, barmaids—women who work in the service industry?

Shy Guys tend to gravitate toward waitresses and hostesses, for one simple reason—it's the easy thing to do. Think about it. These girls are paid to be nice to you. No matter how much they may dislike you personally, they still have to smile and answer all your annoying questions.

When I first started chasing girls, I went after quite a few women in the service industry. Hey, you can't blame a Shy Guy for going for the pretty girl who smiles at you when you walk in the door and makes pleasant conversation while she helps you out.

Am I saying you shouldn't go after waitresses and hostesses? Not at all. Waitresses need love, too, and some of them are very nice. But keep in mind that an attractive waitress gets hit on by a million guys a night, and the bottom line is that she is paid to be nice to you. A lot of Shy Guys mistake professional courtesy for genuine interest. Just because a waitress smiles at you when she brings you drinks doesn't mean she likes you. That's her job, stupid!

I recommend that Shy Guys start with waitresses, and then move on to girls who aren't talking to you just because they want a good tip. If you're serious about overcoming your shyness, you can't just go for the easy marks. You've got to go for a challenge.

And that means not always taking the safest option. Most Shy Guys spend their whole lives doing the thing that is safest, the thing that involves the least amount of risk. (I used to be a bartender, and I've seen a lot of guys who come in and flirt with the waitress all night, without ever making a real effort to get her phone number or ask her out. These guys usually wind up going home alone. If you want to be one of these pathetic guys, that's your business, but don't expect to ever get married.)

The gym is a good place to meet girls, in theory, but it can be tricky. Most girls seem to work out with friends—often their boyfriends—and it can be hard to find a female exercising by herself.

However, the next time you see a girl walking on a treadmill or biking on a Lifecycle, it couldn't hurt to place yourself on the machine next to hers and strike up a little conversation. Pretend you don't know how to operate the machine and ask for some assistance. If nothing else, you know that she likes to exercise, so right off the bat, you have something in common with her. If she seems to be having problems working a machine, then by all means, offer your assistance.

Another idea is to sign up for some aerobics classes, which are generally filled with females. However, you'd better have very strong legs if you're going to employ this technique. I tried it once, and let me tell you, aerobics is brutal on the lower body. Women tend to be much stronger in their lower body than men are; they're built to take this kind of punishment. Men are not!

Legend has it that the supermarket is the ultimate meeting spot. I have my doubts about that. The problem I have with the grocery store as a pickup spot is that girls go to the supermarket for a reason—to buy food in a quick and efficient fashion—and if you are standing in the aisle, trying to put the moves on them, you are just an obstacle in their way.

In a bar or at a party, women expect guys to come on to them. It is a social setting. There is very little to do in a bar besides drink and talk to people, so it seems a little more natural to engage in conversation with strangers.

If you do decide to try the supermarket route, the first thing I recommend is that you check for the ol' wedding or engagement ring. You can save yourself a lot of grief this way.

One advantage of approaching a girl in a supermarket is that it is nice and quiet, so you can actually have a conversation, and there is no competition. The acceptable way of approaching a girl in a supermarket is to pretend you don't know where something is. (Surprise, surprise!)

Ask a girl where you can find the item. Make a comment about how difficult it is for you to find things in the store. Try to make it sound like you just broke up with your girlfriend and haven't had to do much of your own shopping lately. Pretend you just moved into the area.

I think your best bet in the supermarket is to stand behind a cute girl at the checkout line. Make some comment about her food purchases, "Hey, you eat Ho-Hos, too!" or "Oh, man—Cocoa Puffs—I'm really cuckoo for those things!" If she is buying some food you have never tried before, ask her how it is. Point to some tabloids on the rack and make a funny comment about one of the headlines: "Can you believe it? Liz Taylor was kidnapped by UFOs again!" If the line at the checkout lane is long enough, you may have enough time to close the deal.

I once heard a woman say that every time she goes shopping, guys ask her where to find certain food items. The woman was amazed that guys can never find anything in the supermarket. What she didn't realize was that those guys knew exactly where those items were. They were just putting the moves on her.

So it just goes to show you, no matter how unoriginal or uninspired your opening line may be, there's always going to be someone who has never heard it before.

What about the Highway Pickup? That's a pretty popular way to meet someone, right? You're driving down the highway; you pull up alongside a pretty girl; you ask her to follow you as you pull off at the next rest stop. To be honest, I think this method is a little bold for a Shy Guy. It seems more like something a serial killer would do. And while there is a great void in the area of books on effective serial killing techniques, this is not that book. So I'd avoid trying to initiate conversations while you're speeding down the highway. A Shy Guy really works best in situations where he can speak to a girl and let his personality come out. This doesn't work too well at fifty-five miles per hour.

One approach I do recommend is to become a regular customer someplace where girls are known to go. It doesn't matter where it is—a bar, a pool hall, a coffee shop. Go there on a regular basis. Establish a presence there. Bring your friends with you. Get to know the staff on a first-name basis. Make a ritual out of going there every week on the same night, if you want.

Don't expect to meet a girl every time you go there. It should be a place that you enjoy going with your friends to have a good time, whether you hook up with chicks or not. You want to feel comfortable there. Then, when a cute girl does come in, you will have the home court advantage. Never underestimate the advantage of playing on your home turf. Look how important it is in sports.

If you are a regular in a coffee shop, for instance, you come to see the coffee shop as your home away from home. You are very relaxed there, and this will make you more confident in meeting women. They will sense how comfortable you are there, and how well you get along with your friends. Because you are in familiar surroundings, you will be able to show more of your personality and thus, better increase your chance of closing a deal.

You may have to go to the same coffee shop a hundred times before you meet someone, but eventually, all those hours spent establishing your presence will pay off. The more times you go to the same place, the greater your odds of meeting a girl there. The percentages are on your side.

So the next time you and your friends are trying to figure out where to go, just go "where everybody knows your name."

Divide and Conquer

Fact: Pretty girls do not go out alone.

This is one of the rules of being a girl, along with wrapping a towel around your butt at the beach, having a can of Diet Coke with you whenever you drive anywhere, and hating the Three Stooges.

Girls always go out bar-hopping with their friends, often in large groups. This presents a problem for the reader of this book. If you are a true Shy Guy, one thing you never want to do is approach a girl who is with a large group of people. Your best bet is to pick the one girl in the group you are most attracted to, and wait until you can talk to her alone. The question then becomes: How can you get her away from her friends?

There are a number of ways you can accomplish this. One way is to wait until she goes to the bar to get a drink. At that moment, you should go up to the bar and position yourself right next to her.

A good line here is to say something like, "That's a really interesting-looking drink. What is it?" If it's something really exotic, ask the girl what kind of liquor is in it. Often a girl will have an interesting story about how she discovered this particular drink. She might say something like, "I was on vacation in the Bahamas and the bartender kept pushing these Bahama Mamas on us. I got so drunk, blah blah blah."

Of course, if the girl is just drinking an ordinary beer, you'll need to try a different approach. Somehow, "That's a really interesting-looking bottle of beer" just doesn't cut it. However, if the girl is drinking a brand-new beer that is just becoming popular, you might want to ask her how she likes it. Zima and Ice beer both provided good icebreakers when they first came out.

Another suggestion for getting your girl alone is to wait by the entrance to the ladies' room. You figure your girl has to go to the bathroom sometime, and when she does, you'll be waiting to catch her on the way out! (I wouldn't recommend stopping a girl on her way *in* to the ladies' room, because she may be in a hurry and have to cut your conversation short.)

Now, you don't want to stand too close to the ladies' room, because all the other girls in the club will think you're some kind of ladies'–room-stalking freak. About twenty feet away should do nicely.

A better bet is if a bunch of girls go to the ladies' room, and the girl you like stays behind. This may be the only window of opportunity you get, so you'll want to take advantage of that. You only have a few minutes before her friends come back, so you'll have to work fast.

A third approach to use when dealing with a big group of girls is to position yourself next to the one you like best. Stand on the opposite side from where her friends are. Then, when there is a lull in the conversation, give her a gentle tap on the shoulder so she has to turn and face you. (Always wait for that conversational lull. A Shy Guy never interrupts!)

Most clubs are pretty loud, so chances are, no one else can hear your conversation except you and your girl. (A Shy Guy can't stand the thought of anyone eavesdropping on his attempted pickup.)

Talk to your girl for a few minutes, and see if she is interested, or if she's in a hurry to turn back toward her friends. If she gives you her undivided attention, she is interested in you. If she turns her back on you, she is probably not interested.

However, this is not a hard and fast rule. Sometimes you just have to be a little persistent. If a girl turns her back on me, I will sometimes tap her on the arm one more time and attempt further conversation. If she turns away again, then I will take the hint and walk away. If she shows you her back twice, obviously she's not interested. Girls are very good at turning their backs on guys they're not interested in.

Sometimes a girl just wants to hang out with her friends, and doesn't want to be bothered by some strange guy trying to pick her up. But do not take it personally if the girl rejects you. It is entirely possible that she has a boyfriend. It may even be that she simply is not attracted to you. Hey, it happens! The odds of two people being attracted to each other are pretty slim. You may have to kiss a lot of frogs before you find your princess.

The important thing is that you try. And go for high numbers. If you go out, get rejected by one girl, and then call it a night, you will never get very far. I recommend going for the "Three Strikes, You're Out" approach.

Try to hit on at least three girls a night. If you get shot down three times in a row, maybe it's just not your night, and it's time to move on to a new location. Sometimes, you will get lucky and hit it off with a girl your first time at bat. Other times, you may go into a slump and strike out again and again.

The important thing is not to be discouraged. There are so many girls in the world, you're bound to find one eventually.

The Divide and Conquer technique is a good way to single out the girl you like and focus on her. A word of warning, though: some Shy Guys like to pick out the girl they like, and then stand and stare at her all night. This only makes the girl think you are some kind of psycho.

If you stare at a girl for more than five minutes without talking to her, she will probably be so scared of you that you will have absolutely no chance with her. Some Shy Guys like to think they are being "silent and mysterious," when in fact, girls see them as "obsessive and creepy."

The most important thing for a Shy Guy is to make sure you talk to your girl when she is alone. If you try and engage more than one girl in conversation at a time, the girls will not know which one of them you are interested in. When the end of the night comes, all you can do is bid a friendly farewell to both of them, because you didn't single out the one you wanted and ask her for her phone number.

Another technique is to have your buddies distract a girl's friends while you work on the one you like. Who knows? Maybe one of your friends will hook up, too. I call this the Starsky and Hutch technique. When Starsky is about to break into a den of drug dealers and make a bust, does he do it alone? No. He always has Hutch there to back him up. It's the same thing with flirting. To a Shy Guy, approaching a group of babes is the emotional equivalent of entering a den of crack addicts. The adrenaline is pumping, the heart is pounding. It can be a little scary! You need one of your friends to be the Hutch to your Starsky.

In order for this to work, you need friends who are willing to talk to any girl, regardless of whether they find her attractive, to back you up. And you'd better be prepared to do the same for your friends. We're all in this together, guys! We've got to back each other up! Tonight, your friend may ask you to chat up some Rosie O'Donnell look-alike. Tomorrow, you'll get the sex goddess and he'll take the ugly duckling. It all evens out in the end.

Some guys refuse to play the role of "Johnny Ugly Friend," because they don't want to get stuck with a girl they're not interested in. Hopefully, your friends will be more supportive. Besides, as the 1991 movie *Dogfight* shows us, sometimes you start off with a girl you think is a bow-wow, but by the end of the night, she's just a "Wow!"

Shy Guys Don't Pounce

You're in a bar. You see a girl get in an argument with her boyfriend. You see the boyfriend get pissed off and leave. The girl stays at the bar, in tears. What do you do?

If you're most guys, you pounce! If you're a Shy Guy, you go shoot pool with your friends.

You're in line in a fast-food joint. The pretty girl in front of you doesn't have enough money to pay for her food. What do you do?

You pounce and offer her your spare change! Or, if you're a Shy Guy, you keep munching on your fries.

You're coming out of the mall. You see a girl in the parking lot having trouble carrying all her packages. What do you do?

You pounce and offer to help carry her bags! Or, if you're a Shy Guy, you keep on walking.

You're driving down the highway. You see a cute girl along the side of the road. Her car has broken down. What do you do?

You pull over and offer to let her use your cell phone! Or, if you're a Shy Guy, you drive by, thinking about what could have been.

Perhaps you can sense the pattern emerging here. The word "pounce" is not part of a Shy Guy's vocabulary. Pouncing involves confidence. It involves quick action. It involves being able to instantly assess an opportunity and act upon it, like a lion surprising a lone zebra down at the ol' watering hole.

Shy Guys like to take their time, gathering the courage to act. The problem is, while you are trying to get up your nerve, other guys may be moving in on your prey. If you don't learn to act quickly, you'll be left standing there with your hands in your pockets, while some other guy walks off with the girl who should have been yours.

One thing you may have noticed while reading through my various theories on approaching girls is that there is a distinct lack of spontaneity in my suggestions. Take it from a very unspontaneous guy: Shy Guys are not exactly famous for their ability to see a situation and jump on it. Shy Guys like to analyze a situation, evaluate their chances, and wait until just the right opening presents itself. They spend all night psyching themselves up, waiting for just the right time to act. They tell themselves, "After this song, I'll go talk to her. After I finish this drink, I'll go talk to her. I'll go to the bathroom first, then I'll talk to her!"

Usually, by the time a Shy Guy is ready to act, it is too late.

Another thing Shy Guys are not very good at is the Chase. This is when a pretty girl walks by and you run after her, catch up, and talk to her. One thing I always admired in movies is when a character will see a girl he is so attracted to that he will run for six blocks to catch up to her.

A Shy Guy just isn't capable of that kind of effort. Because the Shy Guy is looking for any excuse to not approach a girl. Once a girl has walked past him, he has already given her up for lost. The Shy Guy will talk himself out of making any kind of pursuit. He will say, "I wanted to talk to her, but she walked away before I had a chance. Oh, well. What are you gonna do?"

This is the kind of thinking that holds a Shy Guy back. It is important for the Shy Guy to realize that some things in life are worth working for. Meeting girls is not always easy. Sometimes you really do have to put some effort into it, as you would anything in life that is important to you.

Basically, the Shy Guy is afraid of making a spectacle of himself. What if he chased a girl for blocks, only to get rejected? Better to remain stationary and avoid potential embarrassment.

This also happens when the Shy Guy is in his car. Often, when you are out driving, you will be parked next to a pretty girl at a traffic light. This is a great opportunity for you to strike up a conversation. Instead, most Shy Guys will just sit there and watch impotently as she drives away. Over the years, the Automobile Pickup has become a time-honored way for two people to meet each other. All you have to do is playfully chase her for a few blocks, try to get her to yell out her number, or tell her, "Pull into that parking lot! I want to talk to you!" Unfortunately, Shy Guys just aren't daring enough to participate in the Chase. They are much better at doing the postgame commentary, the Sunday morning wrap-up of "Things I Coulda/Shoulda Said."

Wherever you go, you are going to face competition from pickup artists who are the exact opposite of Shy Guys—Aggressive Guys. They tend to be cocky, arrogant, and extremely forward when it comes to approaching girls. They can be recognized by their complete fearlessness when it comes to pursuing members of the opposite sex.

Aggressive Guys are also known for being very disrespectful to women. They are crude, pushy, and unbelievably persistent. They get a lot of rejections, but because they hit on every girl they see, they get a lot of acceptances, too.

As much as I may despise the Aggressive Guys for their methods and disrespect for women, there is one thing I do have to admire about them: their fearlessness. Where an Aggressive Guy (or A.G.) acts, a Shy Guy observes. Where an A.G. says exactly what's on his mind, a Shy Guy keeps everything to himself. While an A.G. goes after everything in a skirt, a Shy Guy hesitates, letting countless opportunities go by.

There is something to be said for boldness. Now, as I said, the A.G.s often are not very effective in their methods. They sometimes wind up getting shot down by dozens of girls a night. As each girl walks away, A.G.s usually turn on them, calling them nasty names, and making sexist comments.

As much as I may loathe the A.G.s, I must admit there are times when I wish I had their boldness. If an A.G. sees five girls sitting at a table, he will pull a chair up to their table and work on all five girls at once. A typical A.G. come-on is something along the lines of, "You da most beautifulest-lookin' thing I seen all night." Or, "Could we innarest youse in a coupla beers?"

As you might imagine, girls are generally not impressed by this type of guy. But some girls are attracted to an aggressive personality, and the A.G.s do tend to go for high numbers, which works in their favor. This puts the Shy Guy at a disadvantage. You're competing against guys who are far more experienced at this than you are, and far more persistent.

That's why I think it couldn't hurt for a Shy Guy to adopt some of the A.G. philosophy. Don't copy their methods, but take inspiration from their boldness. Whenever I find myself in a situation where no Shy Guy could possibly succeed, I think to myself, "What would an Aggressive Guy do?" Sometimes this gives me the confidence I need to follow through. I tell myself, anything an A.G. can do, I can do better.

After all, you know you are better than those uneducated muscleheads. Why should they get all the girls instead of you, just because they try harder? I think there is something to be learned from our less evolved competition. Just as man can study animals and learn from their behavior, so can we benefit from studying the ways of the Aggressive Guy.

I'm not suggesting you become as crude, cocky, or disrespectful as an A.G., but if you can develop some of their confidence, it will help you a lot in the long run. A little boldness goes a long way. Although the Aggressive Guy is our enemy, we can learn from him, and use his methods against him.

The Best Girls to Approach

One thing I want you to realize is that a Shy Guy is not going to be able to take advantage of every situation. By the very nature of your shyness, there will be times when you are just not comfortable meeting somebody new.

What I'd like to stress here is that a Shy Guy should only approach girls in situations where he feels most comfortable. In most cases this means approaching girls who are alone. This brings up the question: where do you find these girls by themselves? In a bar?

Not likely. No attractive girl ever goes to a bar by herself. It's just not done.

If you do see a pretty girl in a bar, and she appears to be by herself, wait a while and see what happens. Chances are, she's waiting for her friends or her boyfriend. There's also a strong possibility she's dating the bartender. Keep a close eye on her and study her body language. Think of yourself as a cop on a stakeout. You've got to keep the suspect under surveillance before you make the bust. But you must do it discreetly; if she suspects you're watching her, you'll tip her off too soon, and she'll make a clean getaway.

Pay attention to what's going on around her. Is the bartender giving her lots of special attention? Is he giving her lots of free shots and drinks? If so, you probably don't want to pursue her, because she's already taken. A Shy Guy never pursues another man's girl.

Now, there is the occasional case of a girl who is supposed to meet her friends in a bar, but her friends don't show up. This is a great opportunity for a Shy Guy to move in. Look for a girl who seems lost—like she's looking for someone. Ask her who she's looking for. This is a great icebreaker, because it gives the girl a chance to tell her story to someone. No girl likes to be alone in a bar, so by attaching herself to you, she feels little safer. (All Shy Guys have that aura of harmlessness that the ladies find so endearing!) You're keeping her protected from all the scavengers in the bar who would prey on helpless females.

She may even come to look at you as her savior, the one who rescued her from a night of hanging out by herself. I call this the Good Samaritan Approach. It involves creating the illusion that you're there to help her, to lend a sympathetic ear, when, in fact, you're trying to put the moves on her, just like every other guy in the club! The only difference is that you are, hopefully, being more subtle about it than the other guys. No Shy Guy has ever been accused of coming on too strong.

One good thing to do in this situation is to offer to help the girl look for her friends. Of course, never having seen her friends before, there's really no way you can help. Even if she describes her friends to you, odds are she'll spot them before you do, if they ever show up at all.

A few words of warning: If you see a girl who goes to a bar alone, and just sits at the bar and drinks all night until she can hardly stand up straight, she is probably a booze hag. You should avoid her, unless that's the kind of woman you're looking for. And, as we established earlier, any girl by herself who is watching a band is most likely dating one of the guys in the band. No matter how attractive she is, you're better off not talking to her. You'll only get your hopes up for nothing.

Okay, so we've established that a bar is not the best place to meet a solo girl. So what is the best place?

Again, I'd have to go with the beach. Your best bet is to go on weekdays, if at all possible. On weekends, girls tend to go with their friends. But during the week, a girl (especially a college student) is likely to go by herself, since her friends are working or in school, and can't take time off.

Just because you see a girl sitting alone on a towel does not necessarily mean she is alone. You always want to check and see if there is a second towel next to hers. If you see towel number two, wait and see who it belongs to before you do anything. It may belong to a girlfriend of hers, or it may belong to a guy, but you can save yourself a lot of embarrassment by looking before you leap.

When you first walk onto the beach, you may notice a girl by herself right off the bat. Once you have determined that there is no second towel (i.e., no boyfriend present) you may decide to do what most single guys do at the beach—plop down right next to her.

Isn't this a bit obvious? Well, yes it is. But it's also a good, nonverbal way of establishing interest. Any time a Shy Guy can express his interest without actually making conversation, the meeting process is that much easier. By placing your towel in the vicinity of a cute girl, all you're doing is saying, "Hey, I find you attractive. I want to sit next to you."

If you're lucky, the girl is sleeping when you first arrive, so she doesn't notice you positioning yourself so close to her. Then when she wakes up, she doesn't realize how carefully you planned the whole thing. Sometimes, if you plan it right, you can position yourself next to an empty towel. Then the girl comes out of the ocean and finds you next to her.

This works very much to your advantage, because you can put up an act like, "I just happened to be sitting next to this empty towel. I had no idea it belonged to a pretty girl." The girl won't suspect that you actually saw her get up and go in the ocean, and positioned yourself accordingly!

Okay, so you're sitting next to a pretty girl on the beach. Now what do you do? Well, one good thing to do is to ask her to watch your stuff while you go swimming. Sometimes, the girl will make First Contact, and ask you to watch her stuff. This builds an instant connection between the two of you, and makes for easy conversation, because the girl is grateful to you when she gets back from her swim. Another possible approach, of course, is that old standby: to ask her for the time.

Other suggestions: You could tell her you forgot your lotion, and ask to borrow hers. Ask her if there are any good restaurants in the area where you can get lunch. Maybe she wants to join you. If you are with your friends, play Frisbee or football nearby her. Show off as much as possible. Do anything to attract her attention. (The classic Peacock Approach—just as the male peacock uses his brightly colored feathers to attract a mate, so does the male pickup artist strut his stuff, doing anything possible to get a girl's attention!) Make sure your friend throws the football so it lands near her. Then go talk to her. Ask her if she'd like to join you in tossing the Frisbee or football around.

If she is reading a book, ask her how she is enjoying it. Some girls will only look up from their book for two seconds, give a quick answer, and go back to reading. These are not girls who want to be bothered.

Other girls like to talk about the books they are reading. I once met a woman reading a John Grisham book, and this led to a lengthy conversation on all the Grisham books and comparisons to the movie versions. Tell her what kind of books you like, and see if you have any favorite authors in common. If she is reading a trashy romance novel, you probably won't have too much to say to her.

If she is reading a text book, ask her where she goes to school, what kind of courses she is taking, etc. You can usually tell after a couple of questions if she is interested in talking to you or if she is eager to get back to her book. Some girls look forward to taking a break from studying, and you will be giving them the perfect excuse.

What about asking a girl to rub suntan lotion on your back? This seems like a great way to meet babes, right? Nah. Not for a Shy Guy. It's a little too physical, too intimate, too daring. That kind of approach may work for Greg Brady, but few Shy Guys are as groovy as Greg Brady. You're better off leaving that kind of approach to aggressive TV actors. Basically, you're walking up to a total stranger and asking them, "Will you rub this lotion all over my body?"

It just doesn't work for a Shy Guy.

If you are sitting next to a girl who has a radio, you may want to comment on a song, or ask her to put a better station on. This brings us to a rather sticky question: What about headphones?

If you see a girl on the beach who is wearing headphones, chances are she does not want to be bothered. She is in her own little world—the headphones help her screen out everything. She is trying to enjoy a day at the beach alone, with no distractions.

Does this mean you should let her have her wish, just leave her alone? Of course not! She wouldn't be lying out on the beach if she didn't want strange guys to talk to her. After all, she could just as easily sit in her own backyard. It helps to go into any situation telling yourself, "The only reason she came here is to meet a guy. That guy may as well be me."

The bold thing to do in this situation is to walk up to the girl and ask her what music she is listening to. This forces her to remove the headphones to answer your question. If you are persistent, you may get her to keep the headphones off and talk to you. If she is not interested in you, she may put the headphones right back on. She may not even remove them at all. This is her little way of saying, "Hey, I'm trying to listen to music, stupid! Stop bothering me!"

So, to answer the headphones question, it really depends on how attracted to the girl you are. If you find her simply irresistible, by all means, approach her anyway. If the phones come off, you may have a shot. If the phones stay on, well, at least you tried.

Often, girls at the beach are on vacation. If you see a group of young ladies with a camera, offer to take their picture. This can lead to a little bit of conversation about where they are from, how long they are on vacation for, if they know all the best places to go, etc. Conversely, if you are hanging out with a bunch of your friends, offer your camera to a pretty girl on a nearby towel and ask her to take your picture. Then attempt to make conversation.

These days, a lot of girls are bringing their cell phones to the beach. It goes without saying that you do not interrupt a girl while she is talking on her cell phone. You wait until she has finished her conversation. Dutter's Rule is that if a girl is talking on the phone, there is a 50 percent probability that she is talking to her boyfriend, so keep that in mind.

My ideal situation for approaching a girl on the beach is this: You see a pretty girl sitting by herself with no book, no Walkman, and no cell phone. She's looking around, people-watching, interested in everything that is going on around her. This girl is probably bored, since she has nothing to entertain her besides the other people on the beach. This girl is ripe for conversation. Even if she has no interest in you at all, she may be willing to chat for a while.

Now, if the girl has positioned herself as far away from the beach crowd as possible, odds are she doesn't want to be bothered. But if she has planted herself right in the center of the most popular spot on the beach, she may be looking for a little companionship.

I find girls tend to be very friendly at the beach. They are comfortable there. They don't have all their defenses up, like in a bar. The beach is so relaxing that it makes for easy conversation.

But what if you hate the beach, or don't have a beach near you? Well, one of my beach rules also applies to girls in bars. Look for the girls in the bar who are looking around, not really talking to each other. If a girl is constantly moving about the club, not even talking to her friends, it may be that she is looking to meet someone.

If a girl is in motion, wait until she stops before you put the moves on her. Do not, under any circumstances, attempt to stop a girl who is in motion. This is not the Shy Guy way. There is one principle of physics that I understand, and that is this: Bodies in motion stay in motion. Bodies at rest stay at rest. There is not a Shy Guy alive who can alter that equation. If a girl is walking past you with her friends, you would have to be an Ultra-aggressive Guy to get her to stop in her tracks and talk to you. I've seen Ultra-aggressive Guys who will actually grab a girl by the arm and say something along the lines of, "Come here a minute! I want to talk to you!" A Shy Guy is simply not capable of this type of approach. The best a Shy Guy can hope for is to muster a weak "Hi!" as the girl walks by, and hope she noticed him. But that's not going to stop her momentum. No, the Shy Guy's best bet is to wait until the girl has ceased her forward motion—wait and see where she plants herself—and then make his move.

Keep an eye out for a girl who keeps her back to the bar. This is a girl who is looking to meet someone. If she simply wanted to talk to her friends, they would all face the bar, or each other.

Whether in a bar or on the beach, the body language is basically the same. A girl who is seeking a mate will scan the area, looking for someone she finds attractive. She may be with her friends, but follow her eyes. Is she looking at her friends, or is she looking for Mr. Goodbar?

If a girl is locked in a one-on-one conversation with her girlfriend, forget it. You don't stand a chance. Once two girls get into a deep conversation, there's not a guy alive who can pry them apart. You can try, but you've got some tough work ahead of you. Rare is the girl who will abandon a heart-to-heart talk with a fellow female.

Another bad situation is when a group of girls forms a circle. This is a very common scene. As the settlers of the Old West learned over a century ago, putting the wagons in a circle is the most effective way of warding off attacks from Indians. Well, it's the same for girls in a bar. When a group of girls forms a circle, they are protecting each other from the predators in the bar (i.e., the pickup artists). It is extremely difficult and intimidating to break up a circle of girls. Most guys (shy or otherwise) back off from the prospect of trying.

But it is possible. It can be done. Your best bet is to focus on the one you like and try to pull her out of the circle. Look for the one who's not paying attention to the rest of the group, who is not really part of the conversation, who is looking around, checking out all the guys.

Now, what happens if some other guy beats you to the punch and talks to the girl you've had your eye on all night? Well, if you are a Shy Guy, chances are this happens to you a lot. While you're trying to get up the courage to make your move, some Aggressive Guy pounces on your designated girl.

My advice is to wait it out. You have to go out with the attitude that you are better-looking, smarter, funnier, have more personality, whatever, than the loser who is hitting on her now. Once he inevitably gets rejected, because, as we have established, he is a loser, the time will be ripe for you to move in. Your credo must be this: "Every guy other than me is a loser! Every other man will fail, where only I can succeed!"

Often, the really Aggressive Guys are too crude and don't know how to talk to girls. Compared to those guys, you are a saint. Sometimes it works to a Shy Guy's advantage to be the second guy in line to approach a girl. Once the first guy makes a fool of himself with his disrespectful and ignorant ways, you come in and show the girl what a sensitive guy you are. A Shy Guy will almost always look better in comparison to an Aggressive Guy (unless the girl likes disrespectful and ignorant guys, in which case you're out of luck).

Of course, sometimes it works to your disadvantage to come after an aggressive pickup artist. At this point, the girl doesn't want to talk to any other guys, and when you walk in, she's like, "Bring on the next loser!"

Now, if the other guy has spent two hours chatting a girl up, and seems to be doing really well, you may want to move on to another prospect. Don't waste too much time on a girl who is obviously taken. If she starts shoving her tongue down the guy's throat, you may want to reconsider your options.

But if she stops laughing at the guy's jokes and starts looking around the room, that's when all your patience may pay off. Sometimes, after a few minutes of conversation, she decides she wants to see what else is out there. She may pull the old Ladies' Room Ditch. This involves her going to the ladies' room and then sneaking off to some other part of the bar where the guy she was with can't find her.

Once she comes out of the ladies' room, and relocates to a new spot, that's your chance to go over and take a shot. She may then proceed to pull the Ladies' Room Ditch on *you*, in which case, you move on to the next girl. Once a girl has ditched you, don't waste your time pursuing her further. If she wanted to be with you, she would come back to you. End of story.

One other point I want to mention is that just because a girl enters a bar with a guy does not mean she is unavailable. That guy may be her brother, her gay friend, or just a friend. Study their body language. Do they hold hands, kiss, give each other their undivided attention? Or does the guy ignore the girl to watch sports on TV, shoot pool with his friends, or go off and talk to another girl?

Just because a guy and a girl walk into a bar together, doesn't mean they will be leaving together.

Ultimately, the best girls to approach (and this is going to seem rather obvious, but I feel it needs saying) are the ones who look the most approachable. If a girl smiles a lot, seems to enjoy talking to strangers, and has a healthy interest in everything going on around her, she will be much easier for you to talk to than a girl who sits in the corner, stone-faced.

Of course, you can't always tell a girl's personality just by looking at her. You may find yourself pleasantly surprised. Some of the girls who I thought were going to be the most unapproachable turned out to be among the friendliest girls I've met. So it just goes to show you that until you actually talk to a girl, you'll never know what she's really like.

Girls to Avoid

Now that we've covered which girls you should approach, let's take a look at some girls you should stay away from.

1) Married women: You don't want to date a girl who is cheating on someone else to be with you. Even if she ends up divorcing her husband for you, we've already established that she's a cheat, so how could you ever trust her? It may seem exciting to you to get into an affair with a married woman—the forbidden nature of the whole thing—but, ultimately, it's self-defeating to get involved with a woman who's already committed to somebody else. If she gets a divorce, then we can start talking.
2) Biker chicks: I would avoid them, unless you are a biker guy, but I strongly doubt there are many shy biker dudes out there. Biker chicks tend to go for only biker dudes. They like guys who have scars and tattoos. These are dangerous girls who like the feel of hot metal between their legs. Trust me when I say it just wouldn't work out.
3) Booze hags: No matter how attractive she may look with your beer goggles on at two in the morning, you'll come to regret it the morning after. A good rule of thumb: If the girl brags that she can drink any guy under the table, you probably don't want to start thinking long-term here.

4) Illegal aliens who are looking for green cards: Hey, you tell yourself, she may not speak any English, but she will sleep with me every night, and she'll learn to love me! Don't kid yourself. As soon as she learns English, she's gonna get herself a job and she will be outta there. Besides, with communication being the most important thing in any relationship, I really can't stress enough the importance of you and your girlfriend both speaking the same language.
5) Your cousins: This is more of a regional thing. If you're from one of those areas that frowns on dating within your own gene pool, you probably should think about going out with someone who has a different last name than you do. A good rule of thumb is this: First cousins, bad. Second cousins, okay.
6) Underage girls: You would think girls who are sixteen or so would be very impressed by an older guy and would be thrilled to have his attention. Let me tell you something—it does not work that way! Young girls are very intimidated, even frightened by older guys, and they're not afraid to press charges! They know all sorts of big words, like "jailbait" and "statuatory."
7) Girls with serious psychological disorders: Let's say you've been dating a girl for a while and you really like her. Then you find out she's got some serious mental problems. What do you do? First thing I recommend is finding out what type of medication she is on and whether she's taking it regularly. If so, everything may work out fine. If she is off her medication, there could be all sorts of complications which could seriously jeopardize your relationship.
8) Hermaphrodites: Note: Chicks aren't supposed to have dicks! 'Nuff said!

9) Girls who are in prison: George, on *Seinfeld*, thought he had the perfect girlfriend in a female convict. He only had to see her for a few hours a week during visiting hours. But then she was released, and all of George's carefully laid plans fell apart. Those long-distance relationships almost never work out.
10) Lesbians: Face it—they're not interested in you and they're probably not going to let you watch, no matter how much you may fantasize about it! Save yourself a lot of wasted energy and only go after girls who actually like guys! But what about *Chasing Amy*, you ask? That 1997 film had a guy pursuing a lesbian and winning her love! Well, that kind of thing may happen in the movies, but I wouldn't try asking out Ellen DeGeneres. I appreciate a challenge as much as the next guy, but come on.

There is one other type of girl you should avoid. I call her the Sex Goddess. Allow me to explain.

When I first started going out to clubs, I used to look for the best-looking girl in the whole place. The Bombshell. The Stunner. The Knockout. The absolute Beauty Queen. The Center of Everyone's Attention.

I used to get shot down by these girls every time, and then I would call it a night, secure in the knowledge that at least I had gone for the best-looking girl in the place. After a while, I realized that these were not the ideal girls to go for. You see, there are some girls who go out to clubs for one reason only: to make heads turn. (I have to thank my cousin Anna for setting me straight on this one. She gave me the lowdown on the real reason why pretty girls can make life such hell for men.)

For some females, going club-hopping is the ultimate way for them to get attention. They fix their hair up, they put on tons of makeup, they pick out their sexiest outfit, and then they go from bar to bar, frustrating every guy in sight. Some girls really get off on it. It's like a power trip. I once had a girl tell me her idea of a good time is to go out and "use, abuse, and refuse" men. Girls like that really make life frustrating for a Shy Guy (or any guy, for that matter).

It's not necessarily that Sex Goddesses go out with the intention of rejecting every man they meet. It's that they are going out just to be seen. Once they've been seen by everyone in the club, they move on to the next place. Whichever Sex Goddess gets the most attention is the winner. These are girls who like to make an entrance. When they walk into a room, they want every eye in the place to be on them. When they dance, they often dance together, for maximum attention, peppering their dances with some really slinky, erotic moves. They may hold hands with each other wherever they go. They may perform pseudo-lesbian moves on each other on the dance floor.

It's all a desperate bid for attention. It's kind of sad, really, if you think about it. If these girls are so shallow that they get off on this kind of attention, they are probably not people you want to know, anyway. If you attempt to talk to these girls, you are only stroking their egos by giving them one more victim to shoot down. You are just setting yourself up for a fall.

Unfortunately, because many Shy Guys have old-fashioned ideas of beauty, Sex Goddesses have a very strong appeal. There's always that one-in-a-million chance that one of these girls could take a liking to a Shy Guy, so I suppose they're worth a token effort, if you feel you must. But don't knock yourself out.

Do it fast. Get in line, make your pitch, and get out. There are plenty of other pathetic guys waiting in line behind you for their chance to get shot down. At least you can say you talked to the best-looking girl in the club. But once you're done with that little diversion, it's time to come back to Earth and go after girls that are actually attainable.

I'm not saying you can't get one of these Sex Goddesses. I'm just saying, generally the Sex Goddesses are not looking to get picked by anyone—I repeat, anyone! Even if Tom Cruise were in the bar, they would laugh at him before turning their backs on him and heading out onto the dance floor. These girls are just out to have a good time dancing with each other, rejecting men, and getting attention.

It is one of the sad facts of nightclub life that the girls who are the most attractive are very often the most inaccessible. (There is nothing worse in life than a hot girl who *knows* she is hot. Far better to find that rarer creature, the hot girl who *doesn't* know what a great prize she is!) You can save yourself a lot of grief if you just enjoy the Sex Goddesses from afar. That's the way they prefer to be enjoyed. In fact, they usually try to avoid conversation with every guy in the club.

This is one of the reasons I actually recommend bars over clubs. I find people who go to bars tend to be more real, more accessible. People who go to clubs tend to be more superficial, more concerned with being seen than meeting someone.

Sex Goddess are a very frustrating part of nightclub life. It always amazes me how a girl can dress herself up like a Penthouse Pet and then appear annoyed that men would actually want to talk to her! They always get that pissed-off look, as if to say, "Just because I'm wearing a skin-tight dress with an ultra-short skirt, and my boobs are hanging out, doesn't mean I'm trying to attract a man!" No, they really are not trying to attract *a* man—they're trying to attract *every* man. They want all these men to *look* at them, but not actually *talk* to them! They are Untouchable.

Believe me when I tell you, the Sex Goddesses do not want to be bothered.

Dreaming of a Dream Girl!

Every Shy Guy likes to think he is going to end up with a Playboy Playmate. Sadly, this is not the case. It's a hard reality to accept, but odds are that if you're basically a shy person at heart, you're not going to end up with Miss September. You may want to lower your expectations to a slightly more realistic level.

Lowering one's standards is a hard thing for Shy Guys to do. Many Shy Guys subscribe to the Hollywood idea of glamour. We like our girlfriends to be very feminine, long-haired, lotsa-makeup wearing, non-sports-watching, soft-voiced, smooth-skinned, dress-wearing, old-fashioned girls. In short, we like our girls to be girlish.

Generally, a Shy Guy places such a high value on finding his Dream Girl that he is not willing to accept anything less. A classic example of this type of behavior is found on the TV series *Seinfeld*, in which the characters of Jerry and George are so heartless and shallow that they will find any excuse to dump a girl. Maybe she wears the same outfit every day. Maybe she likes Dockers commericals. Whatever. It doesn't matter. They will never rest until they find a girl who is perfect. This is why Jerry and George are still single after all these years.

My old pal, Kerwin McLachlan, likes to say that a man can find a flaw in even the most perfect woman. If you were dating Cindy Crawford, you would think to yourself, "Yeah, she's beautiful, but too bad about that mole . . . Isn't there something she can do about that?"

Shy Guys tend to be notoriously picky when it comes to girls. We have incredibly high standards, because of a lifetime spent making love to *Playboy* centerfolds and Hollywood's hottest starlets. (Well, photos and videotapes of centerfolds and actresses, anyway, but you get the idea!)

Even though we spend our whole lives looking for a girl to match that picture we have in our heads, the sad fact is that, unless you're Scott Baio, most guys never find their Dream Girl—ever. We all have two versions of the perfect girl in our heads. First, there is what I like to call Fantasy Girl. She is every man's ultimate woman, physically. She is the epitome of what you are looking for. Then there is Reality Girl. She is who you end up with. She is not perfect, any more than you and I are.

There is nothing wrong with having a picture in your head of your Fantasy Girl, as long as you accept the reality that you are never going to get her. You may come close—you may meet someone with some of the qualities you look for—but no one is perfect.

When most guys describe their ideal woman to me, they usually describe someone who is the exact opposite of the girl they have now.

A guy who has a flat-chested wife will say he likes big breasts. A guy who is dating a blonde wants a brunette. A guy who has an American girlfriend fantasizes about an Asian girl. And there is nothing wrong with this. It is perfectly healthy to have an active fantasy life. The mistake most Shy Guys make is that they are looking for a Fantasy Girl in real life.

I have a friend who likes to think he can change girls, to transform Reality Girl into Fantasy Girl. If he is attracted to a girl who is overweight, he'll comment to me that she can always have liposuction. If he likes a girl who has a big nose, he'll note that she can always get a nose job. If she has extremely short hair, he'll remark that she can always grow it. If she has a mustache, he says she can shave it off.

The problem with this line of thinking is that you are not attracted to the girl as she is—you're attracted to some idea of what she could be. This isn't fair to her and it isn't fair to you. Go for a girl that appeals to you as she is now.

It is naive to think that you can change someone. I'm not saying it's impossible, but it is wrong to go into a relationship planning to do this. If your girl is going to change, it should be because she wants to, not because you want her to. And even if you can get someone to change their physical appearance, you can never get someone to change their personality, so don't even think about trying that one. If some girl has a personality trait that bothers you, you'd better just give up on her now, because it's only going to get a helluva lot more annoying. If she has a bad habit, like smoking, she's going to have to want to give it up on her own. You can't make her quit.

You're better off giving up this unrealistic quest for your Dream Girl. Forget about trying to change a girl into something she's not. You have to learn to accept people for what they have—not for what they might have in the future. I'm sure that most girls wind up married to a guy who is the exact physical opposite of their Dream Man, as well.

Take a good look at yourself. Unless you are a perfect ten, odds are you will not end up dating a girl who is a ten. You need to evaluate how attractive you are, and then find a girl who is on the same level, physically. If you try to date a girl who is out of your league, you will probably be worried constantly about losing her to another guy.

You're better off dating a girl who is your equal. Find a girl who is merely "cute," instead of "drop-dead gorgeous." Let the beautiful people have each other. They belong together. As Jerry

Seinfeld has noted, 90 percent of the people in the world are undateable. Be prepared to end up with one of that 90 percent.

If you keep on looking for that Dream Girl, you're only going to find her in your dreams.

Meeting Girls at School

I never had a date in high school. We've established that. But I know some people who did, and I watched a lot of TV shows starring middle-aged actors going on dates in high school, so I figure that qualifies me as something of an authority. (Back in high school, I was what was known as a *Dukes of Hazzard/Love Boat*-er. That meant you were home on Friday and Saturday nights, watching TV, in case you didn't know!)

One of my friends, Tommy, is a classic Shy Guy (he's the guy I mention in my dedication as the inspiration for this book). Despite being just as shy as I was in high school, Tommy still managed to get dates. I asked Tommy what his secret was. How was he able to overcome his affliction and score with chicks while I could only watch Daisy Duke get hit on by Deputy Enos?

Did he ask out the prettiest girls in his class? No, Tommy informed me. That's not the way school works. You never ask out any girls in your class. If the other kids found out, you'd be the laughing stock of the whole class.

Then how, I wondered, was he able to have such a great social life as a teenager? Simple, he told me. He went to parties and met girls from *other* schools. That way, you could ask them out, and no one from your school could give you any guff. Another suggestion of Tommy's was to go for girls who are in different grades from yours. Again, this spares you the humiliation of having everyone in your grade know you've been shot down.

Tommy's high school dating techniques bring up one valid point: a Shy Guy does not ever want to ask out a girl that he must see on a daily basis. In other words, if she's in your class, or you see her at work every day, you're probably better off not going for her.

The reason for this is that if the girl shoots you down, you're going to have to face her every single day. You'll have to go to work or school every morning, knowing that she's there and she has rejected you. You have put your heart on the line for her, revealed to her your most intimate feelings, and found that she is just not interested in you. Now you have to live with that. She knows your greatest secret. She knows you like her. She's probably told everyone else in the school or office. Everyone knows you like her, and that you will never have her.

That's a heavy load for a Shy Guy to bear. Now, if there's a girl you see at work or at school every day that you really like a lot, then by all means go for her, but be prepared to face the consequences. Otherwise, your best bet is to follow my friend's advice and go for girls who are in other grades or attend other schools.

My best advice for meeting girls at school is this: partipate in activities that interest you and see if there are any girls participating in the same activity. Are you into sports? Why not try out for a team? Particularly one where there are boys and girls competing together, such as volleyball or softball. Maybe you can even go after one of the cheerleaders. Oh, wait—this is a book for Shy Guys. Forget I said that.

Are you musically inclined? You may want to join the school band. High school and college bands take lots of long bus rides together, and sometimes play in competitions in far-off cities. This type of road trip is a great way to get to know a girl.

Do you like writing? Why not join the school paper? Another suggestion is to join the yearbook committee, which always has lots of girls on it. Or you could join one of those useless clubs that doesn't ever seem to do anything but every school seems to have—the Key Club. I don't know what the Key Club is or what it does, but every school seems to have one to pad college applications and resumes. There are school clubs for just about every activity you can think of—chess, golf, table tennis, model planes, etc.

Does your school sponsor any trips to Broadway plays or amusement parks? This could be a good way to meet a girl you have something in common with. Does your school sponsor any ski trips? Why not sign up for one? You never know what can happen. It could be a good opportunity for you to be alone with that cute girl you pass in the hallway every day.

Are you interested in acting? Why not try out for a school play? This is a great opportunity for you to be around lots of girls. Maybe you'll even get to do a kissing scene with an aspiring young starlet, and you'll have to rehearse it over and over again. Do you like to draw? Maybe there will be a cute model in your art class. Are you into photography? Maybe you can ask a pretty girl to pose for you—and you know where that's gonna lead!

How about signing up for a class where there are traditionally a lot of girls, like home economics, sewing, or typing?

If you are really serious about pursuing girls, you may want to consider taking classes to become a teacher yourself. These classes are often filled with women! My friend Bill decided that becoming a schoolteacher was the most logical way to meet girls, so he signed up for education classes in college. Often, he was the only guy in a class filled with chicks! Was this guy smart, or what? He wound up marrying one of the girls he went to school with. The perfect crime!

Do you like politics? You may wish to run for student office. You may not win the election, but marching on the campaign trail is a can't-miss way to meet girls. (Hey, it works for Bill Clinton!)

Is there a girl in your math class you like, but can't get up the nerve to talk to? Why not offer to tutor her, or ask her to tutor you? Even if you are a brilliant math student, you can pretend to be an idiot. Think of it as playing Ultimate Clueless Boy. If there's one thing TV has taught me, it's that a private tutoring session often leads to a serious smooching session! You start off with a little math homework, and the next thing you know, you're studying some other subjects instead—like human biology and anatomy. (Wink, wink! Nudge, nudge!)

If you are in college, you might want to join a fraternity—a great way to meet sorority sisters. Never turn down an invitation to a party. You may wish to join some student organizations. How about the freshmen orientation committee? That's a great way to meet the hot new chicks. You'll have first crack at them, and they'll trust you because you're the first person they'll meet on campus.

Most Shy Guys really come into their own in college. That's usually the first time a Shy Guy gets laid. My friend Hugo is the classic case of the quiet guy who blossomed in college. When Hugo was in high school, he kept pretty much to himself. He didn't date, and he never went out. He was content to spend most of his nights at home watching TV or playing video games.

When Hugo went to college, he gradually began to come out of his shell. He made more friends and started going to parties. Eventually he became one of the most popular guys in his dorm. The next thing you knew, Hugo had a steady girlfriend and was having sex for the first time in his life.

All of this came about because he had left the cocoon of his parents' house and gone out into the world. For a Shy Guy, going away to college is a very scary thing. It's also the best thing that could ever happen. It means leaving that nice, safe, comfortable nest you grew up in, and facing the unpredictable. Believe me, it is a move well worth making. If you are basically a quiet guy who doesn't get out much, college will give you enough experiences to last a lifetime. Heck, I only went to a local community college, and I was still able to ask out my first girl there.

I like to say that I went to college to major in life experience, and that's exactly what I did.

Meeting Girls at Work

Meeting women at work is a lot like meeting girls at school. No matter what happens, you will have to see them every day, so you have to be careful. There are no secrets in a workplace environment. Everyone tells everyone *everything*—and I do mean everything.

Anyone who thinks he can keep a secret in a work setting is only fooling himself. As soon as more than one person knows something, the whole office knows it. This is true whether you work at McDonald's or in a top Madison Avenue advertising firm. People are basically the same wherever you go, and nothing brightens up the average workday like hearing some juicy gossip about a co-worker.

If you date a co-worker, you will be the talk of the office. Remember *Cheers*, when Sam was dating Diane? The whole bar knew their business! Don't think for a minute that you will fall beneath the office radar. The minute anyone in an office makes the slightest romantic move, it instantly becomes the hot topic of everyone's E-mail.

So if you are thinking of taking the plunge into a workplace romance, take that into account. You will be in the spotlight, and it's a spotlight that can burn with white-hot intensity. You will be the center of the office universe. Everything you and your girl say and do will be duly noted, logged, and recorded by your fellow staffers. In a sense, it's as if you're dating the entire office.

Now, if you can put up with this kind of intense scrutiny, that's great. If you don't mind living under a corporate microscope, fine. Some people can deal with it. I'm just trying to warn you that there can be unwanted consequences—the kind that can cause great mental anguish to a Shy Guy.

Ultimately, of course, it doesn't matter what anybody thinks except you and the girl you are dating. If you enjoy each other's company and want to continue seeing each other, then by all means, do so. What you and your woman do is nobody else's business anyway.

Don't forget though, that if the romance ends, you'll still have to see each other five days a week, eight hours a day. Perhaps even work alongside each other. If the girl has rejected you, this will be agonizing. Imagine being so close to her that you could reach out and touch her—remembering what once was—and knowing that you will never have her again.

Shy Guys often pin a lot of hope on a girl, and if the relationship doesn't work out, they generally don't want to see her again. Seeing her forty hours a week, or more, and knowing she wants nothing to do with them, well, that's quite a burden to bear, let me tell you. (Of course, if there's a girl in your office who you have a huge crush on, and it's tearing you up inside, by all means, pursue her. Better to get shot down like a man than to go through life afraid of rejection.)

Personally, I wouldn't recommend a workplace romance for a Shy Guy. It just causes too much unnecessary grief. It's hard enough for two people to get together in this crazy world of ours. You don't need a bunch of busybodies watching over your affair.

There is one exception, however: If you are planning on quitting your job soon, or if the girl is planning to quit soon, it's open season. It doesn't matter what happens, since you will not be dealing with each other on a daily basis, and the two of you will no longer be under the gaze of your curious co-workers. If you find out a girl in your office will be leaving soon, that's when you want to make your move. Time it to coincide with her final days in the office. Just don't keep putting it off until her going away party. By then, it may be too late.

Now, let's say you're willing to deal with the consequences of the workplace romance. You've decided you can live with the dirt-dishing by your co-workers, and the prospect of having to face her every day, even if it doesn't work out. How do you initiate an office romance?

Usually, the Shy Guy approach is to avoid the girl as much as humanly possible. When a Shy Guy is attracted to a girl he works with, he is usually so afraid of anyone, especially her, finding out that he goes out of his way to make sure he never sees her. Surprisingly, this method of "playing hard to get" is usually not too effective. Believe it or not, you need to actually give the girl some clues that you're interested. Fortunately, this is not as hard as it may seem.

For starters, do your co-workers get together and go out a lot after work? If so, this could be a good opportunity to get to know your girl in a relaxed atmosphere. Start tagging along on these after-work gatherings. Always make sure you sit close to the girl you like and give her your undivided attention.

After a few of these outings, if she seems to get along with you pretty well, start suggesting the two of you go off and do your own thing sometime. Something nonthreatening. A movie. A concert. Try to arrange it so the two of you can spend as much time as possible alone together.

Does she need a ride home from work? Make sure you are the

one to give it to her every night. Even if you have to go miles out of your way, play it off like it's no big deal. She will come to think of you as a really nice guy who is very supportive of his co-workers.

Start going out to lunch with her—just the two of you. See if it leads to anything. Invite her out for a couple of drinks after work, or a cup of coffee at the local coffee shop. She will trust you, feel safe around you, because she knows you from the office. If she had met you on the street, she might not have given you the time of day.

One technique you might want to try is to use office gossip to your advantage. Gossip can be a dangerous weapon, but it can also be a helpful tool, if used properly. Here's how it works. Say there's a co-worker you work with whom you are attracted to, but you're not sure how she feels about you.

All you have to do is to tell just one of your co-workers about your feelings for this woman, and word will spread like wildfire. In no time at all, you will find out if you have any chance at all. It will be as if you had gone up to her and told her yourself. It's sort of the office equivalent to passing a note in gym class. To ensure swift results with this method, be sure to use the phrase, "Don't tell *anyone*" when you confess your intentions to your trusted co-worker.

Does your workplace sponsor any group events? It's not a bad idea to sign up for ski trips, softball games, corporate marathons, or other group activities. As a Shy Guy, I've spent a lifetime avoiding group activities. My feeling has always been: the more people that are going, the less likely that I will. I prefer to interact with as few people as humanly possible.

You may feel the same way I do. You're probably the guy who goes to a party and tries to find a quiet corner where he can be alone. If so, you may want to consider revising your outlook.

Rebel against the Old Ways of doing things. The Old Ways aren't working too well for you, or you wouldn't be wandering the self-help section of your book store.

Go to some parties. Every office has them, especially around the holidays. Every office has a story of the time that one secretary got really drunk at a party and did something wild. That could be your big chance.

If you don't want to date any women in your office, there is still hope for you. Do you work in a big complex or a strip mall? There may be plenty of other gals in the surrounding buildings. Just like in the previous section, where I advised dating girls from other schools, dating gals from other businesses in the area frees you from a lot of the hangups associated with workplace relationships.

How do you meet these females in the surrounding offices?

One way is to enter one of these other buildings, and pretend you are curious about what kind of work goes on there. Ask a lot of questions of the girl behind the counter. (Corporate Clueless Boy!) You may even stop in several times, getting to know the girl, until you get up the courage to ask her out to lunch.

In the spring and summer, you may be able to eat your lunch outside. This is a great way to meet girls.

Many women smoke cigarettes, and are forbidden to do so in their workplaces. If you are a smoker, you may want to go outside and join them. Most offices have a secret place where the smokers go to light up. Find out where this place is and puff away.

However, if you are not already a smoker, I really can't recommend this course of action. The pursuit of a lifemate is a worthwhile goal, but it's not worth getting lung cancer.

Now, let's say you want to do a little harmless flirting with a woman in your workplace. These days, there is a lot of controversy about sexual harassment. It's unfortunate, but we live in a world where even a friendly come-on in the office can be interpreted as sexual harassment. You can't even compliment a co-worker on her appearance without worrying that you've violated her rights in some way.

So how do you know when you've crossed the line from flirting to sexual harassment? My advice is to play it by ear. Start off with some mild flirtation, and see how she responds to it. Is she receptive? If so, take it further. Does she flirt back with you? Some girls really enjoy flirting, especially with their co-workers. They may have no intention of ever doing anything about it, but a little URST is a healthy way to brighten any office environment.

(That's Unresolved Sexual Tension, for those of you who don't know. URST is the thing that makes office life interesting, and TV shows like *Moonlighting* popular. Once Bruce Willis and Cybill Shepherd actually slept with each other and resolved their sexual tension, the show lost all its appeal. The same thing happened with *Lois & Clark: The New Adventures of Superman*. The producers of the *X-Files*, on the other hand, realize the folly of resolving URST; that is why Scully and Mulder will never have sex.)

If your co-worker is receptive to your initial flirtations, gradually make your flirtations more obvious, until it is painfully apparent to her that you are interested. If she complains to the boss, or tries to get you fired, then you should stop.

The other day I overheard a middle-aged restaurant manager tell his female teenage hostess that he wanted to cover her in chocolate syrup and lick it off. I'd say he crossed the line with that one. I'd advise you to be a little more subtle. Don't reveal your food-related sex fantasies to your officemates. Save that kind of stuff for your wedding night.

And if any of your co-workers sexually harasses you, make sure you report it immediately to their superiors, or file a complaint with somebody! Unless you enjoy it, in which case, just harass them right back.

Hunting for Easy Prey

Okay, you think you're ready to go out on the prowl, but you're still intimidated by girls you are strongly attracted to. This is a common Shy Guy problem. When you finally meet a girl you find incredibly beautiful, you are so tongue-tied that you can't talk to her. So what do you do?

Well, I've made a lot of hunting analogies in this book. Allow me to give another. Let's say you are a lion, prowling through the jungle, looking for a bite to eat. You come across a bunch of gazelles, grazing in a field. As you charge toward them, the swift gazelles scatter, running for their lives.

But one of the gazelles is not quite as swift as the others. This gazelle is wounded; it has a broken leg. You're pretty confident you can catch one of the healthy gazelles—you are King of the Jungle, after all—but that lame gazelle is so helpless . . . such easy prey . . .

Which one do you go for?

It should come as no shock to you that I recommend going for the wounded gazelle. It will take less effort on your part. It will be an easy kill, and you'll be eatin' some tasty gazelle meat in no time.

Let me set a similar scene. You walk into a party. All of the girls are thin, sexy, beautiful—and they all have guys crawling all over them. Then you see one girl in the corner. She is cute, but she's a little heavier than the others. She has glasses. Her clothes are out of style. Her hair is not particularly well-kept. She doesn't exactly stand out in a crowd. She is basically being ignored. This is the one you want to go for.

She is easy prey.

If you go for a perfect girl, you will be competing with every other guy at the party. But if you go for a slightly flawed girl, you will have far less competition, because some guys are not willing to lower their standards. As Homer Simpson's father, Grandpa Simpson, once put it, "Go for the bruised fruit! The dented car!"

You may be pleasantly surprised to find that dating a slightly imperfect-looking girl can be just as satisfying as dating a beauty queen. Often, the more beautiful a girl is, the more of an attitude she has. Girls who are not flawless are usually a lot nicer. So the next time you walk into a bar, why not look for the girl who is like that wounded gazelle down by the watering hole? Maybe she is overweight. Maybe she wears glasses, or has a bad complexion. Maybe her hairstyle is drab, and she's not up on the latest fashions.

Give her a chance. Talk to her; spend a few hours getting to know her; get her phone number. No one says you ever have to use it. But by showing interest in her, by choosing her over all the other, far more glamorous girls around her, you will make her night. For a few brief hours, at least, she will feel special. She will be thrilled that you found her attractive enough to want to meet her. Hopefully she won't figure out the real reason you are talking to her.

As you speak to this Easy Prey, you may get past her looks, and decide you really do like her. The girl often becomes more attractive to you as the night goes on. Sometimes you may think a girl is unattractive when you first see her, but then, as you get to know her, your opinion of her changes to the point where you find her looks offbeat, but strangely appealing. You may even come to appreciate girls with unconventional looks, girls who don't look like they just stepped out of a Victoria's Secret catalog.

One advantage to this approach is that it can be a good confidence-builder. Let's say you go out with your friends one night, and you approach girls that you are mildly attracted to. Then, the next time you go out, you're feeling more confident, so you put the moves on some young ladies you find slightly more attractive. The next time, you go for chicks that are much more your type. And gradually, your confidence increases to the point where you can talk to the girl that you really wanted to talk to all along.

The more girls you approach, the better you will get at it. In no time at all, talking to new girls will be as easy as talking to your own friends. The important thing is that you grow comfortable through experience. Every girl you talk to—even ones you aren't particularly attracted to—will only make you more confident when you talk to the next one. Conversations are like plane crashes: any one you can walk away from is a good one. You can benefit from every conversation you have.

And don't forget—just because a girl is not your type at the beginning of the night, does not mean she won't be your type by the end of the night.

It really is worth it to pursue every girl you have even the slightest interest in. Because you never know when that ugly duckling may surprise you and turn into a beautiful swan.

Chapter Five

Dating in the Electronic Age

In the old days, it was simple. If a girl wanted to blow you off when you called her, all she had to do was say to her mother, "Tell him I'm not home!" Sometimes you'd even hear her whispering in the background, just in case you didn't get the hint.

It was not the most subtle method of rejection, but it got the point across. These days, things are not nearly so primitive. Due to the advances of modern technology, it is now possible for a girl to reject you without ever saying a word. Heck, you're lucky if you even get to talk to her mother. Instead, you usually get the dreaded answering machine!

Yes, the answering machine—the bane of the existence of Shy Guys everywhere. These days, it's almost a given that any time you call anyone, you will get their answering machine. You leave a message with them, they leave a message with you, then you leave a message with them again.

But you never actually talk to each other. It's more like your answering machines are dating each other. It can be very frustrating. You're trying to have a relationship with someone, and all you're really doing is playing phone tag.

What makes things even worse is that many girls screen their calls, picking and choosing who they will talk to. As you might imagine, this puts quite an obstacle in your path when you're trying to start a relationship.

Let me paint a scenario for you. You meet a girl and the two of you really hit it off. You drink, dance, and laugh the night away. You make plans to see each other again. At the end of the night, she gives you her phone number, and a big kiss. Excited about this intriguing new prospect for romance, you give her a call, and get her answering machine. She doesn't return your call. You wait a day or two, then leave another message. Again, she fails to return your call.

Dejected, you realize that her answering machine message is the last time you will ever hear her voice. You start to wonder if she ever got your messages. Maybe they were erased before she got them. Maybe her machine is broken. Maybe someone else in her family heard the messages and forgot to give them to her. You'll never know. You don't even know if the girl is still alive!

Well, odds are she is still alive, and she has heard your messages. She has taken advantage of modern technology to let you know that, for whatever reason, she doesn't ever want to see you again, and you'll never know the reason why.

You can try calling her at work, but odds are you won't get through to her there, either. All you'll do is reach her voice mail.

You can drive yourself crazy, analyzing, trying to figure out what went wrong, but it's not worth the hassle. The bottom line is she's just not interested, and there's nothing you can do to change that. I've said it before; I'll say it again: there are millions of girls out there who want to date you. Why waste your time on one girl who doesn't?

Instead of a phone number, some girls now give out their beeper numbers. Then you're left beeping her, and wondering if she's even getting the beeps. Is she out of range? Has she stopped paying her beeper bill? You'll never know.

Some girls will give you the number of their cellular phones, but those things don't work if the battery has not been charged.

If a girl wants you out of her life, new technology makes it possible so that she never has to speak to you again. With Caller I.D., she can see who is calling her, and, if she chooses, block your line from ever getting through to hers.

If you do call a girl and get her answering machine, the pressure is really on. Shy Guys don't seem to do well when it comes to leaving messages. Usually we talk too long and get cut off before we can give our phone numbers. Then we have to call back and leave a second message, and we feel like idiots.

It's not easy talking to a machine. The machine doesn't talk back, and it's somehow not the same as talking to the girl. You feel like you're auditioning for her, and if she doesn't like the message you leave, you fail the audition. One of the only benefits I can see to constantly getting a girl's answering machine is that it allows you to get in the last word on a relationship gone bad.

And then there's call waiting—don't get me started on that one. Call waiting is my least favorite of all modern technological "conveniences." Call waiting allows the user to take two phone calls at once, and then choose which caller they find more interesting. Talk about humiliating!

There's nothing worse than when you're on the phone with a girl, and she asks you to hold on while she clicks to the other line—and then clicks back to you and tells you to call her later, because she's got someone she'd much rather talk to on the other line. I get very offended when another caller rates higher than me. If a girl is interested in dating you, you should rate higher than anyone else who calls. In fact, I think true love these days is defined as when a girl chooses to stay on the line with you and ignore the other incoming call *completely*.

Sometimes if a girl really doesn't want to talk to you, she will put you on hold and leave you in phone limbo, waiting forever for her to return. Sometimes the girl "forgets" to click back to your line, and you have to call back. Often, girls will use call waiting as a way of blowing a guy off. If she puts you on hold enough times, she figures eventually you'll get the hint that she doesn't want to talk to you. When a girl really hates you, she will tell you she is clicking to another line and then she will hang up on you. All of these approaches are cowardly and cruel and, unfortunately, are used with increasing frequency.

It is almost enough to make one long for the good ol' days of busy signals. I really miss the busy signal. It may have given you an inconclusive answer, but at least it didn't give one human being so much power over another. It's enough to make one nostalgic for the days when, if you liked a girl, you stood outside her balcony and serenaded her, and if she wasn't interested in you, she just poured a big pot of hot oil on you. It may have been painful, but at least it was straightforward.

I prefer not to talk to machines at all. I've actually reached the point where if I call a girl and get three rings, I hang up, because I know the answering machine will click on after the fourth. I'd rather hang up before the machine clicks on. This way, she doesn't know I've called. There's no evidence; no blinking light to incriminate me. It's the perfect crime.

My philosophy is: I'd rather talk to a human being or nothing at all. It's a lot better than pouring your heart out to a machine and then having to stop at the sound of the tone. Just about the only positive thing I have to say about all these new methods of communication is that they work both ways, and that someday the tide will turn and you will be the one screening your calls.

Then you'll be grateful that the answering machine provides a safe buffer zone between you and your unintended.

Cowardly? Yes. Nonconfrontational? You betcha. But hey, we are Shy Guys, after all!

Okay, now it's Pop Quiz time. You meet a girl on a Saturday night, and she gives you her phone number. When do you call her?

a) Sunday morning
b) Monday
c) Tuesday
d) Wednesday

The correct answer to this question is either *c* or *d*. You NEVER want to call a girl the day after meeting her. The movie *Swingers* has a running joke about the tradition of waiting one day before calling someone. One character even decides that since everyone else waits one day, he's going to wait two days from now on, just to be different.

The reason for waiting is that if you call a girl too soon after meeting her, she will think you are desperate. Better to play it cool and lie low for a few days. A lot of Shy Guys are so excited to finally meet a great girl that they get over-anxious and, in their enthusiasm, wind up scaring her away. That's why your best bet is to chill out for a couple days and create a feeling of doubt in the girl's mind.

You'll have her wondering, "Is he going to call, or isn't he?" Then when you finally do call, she'll be that much more interested in talking to you. By avoiding her for a few days, you're creating the impression that you have a full and active life, even if in reality, you were just sitting around staring at the wallpaper. She will think you were just too busy to call her.

After the first date, you can call her as often as you like. In fact, if the date goes well, most girls would probably like to hear from you the next day, just to reassure them that you really do like them. If you wind up having sex with the girl, the next-day phone call is almost mandatory. Girls do not surrender their bodies to every guy that comes along, so if she gives herself up to you, it may mean she really likes you. By calling her the next day, you're letting her know that it meant something to you, too.

Now, a word of warning. Many girls enjoy talking on the phone. A lot. And they're not real picky about who they talk to. In other words, just because a girl spends hours on the phone talking to you, doesn't necessarily mean she likes you. It just means she likes talking on the phone.

The one thing that used to frustrate me the most when I first started dating was girls who would spend hours and hours on the phone with me, even though they had no intention of ever seeing me again. I never understood it. It just didn't make any sense to me. How could a girl be willing to spend an entire evening on the phone with someone, but not be willing to spend five minutes with them in person?

Now that I have the wisdom of my advanced years, I've got a few theories. One is that talking with you on the phone is safe. The girl doesn't have to actually be in the same room with you; thus she frees herself from any sexual obligation. She doesn't have to deal with the possibility of you making a move on her. She doesn't have to kiss you, or worry about you wanting to "go all the way," as they used to say back in the fifties. There is a comfort zone. She has the opportunity of getting to know you better, without having to risk any kind of physical contact.

Another possibility is that she is undecided about whether she really likes you or not. All it takes is a few hours of conversation on the phone to make up her mind. By engaging you in conversation, she is getting you to open up about yourself, and give her all the information she needs to help her decide. She may be on the fence about you, but one wrong word, one slip-up, and bam! You're outta there!

Another possibility is that the girl may just be bored. Having nothing better to do, she doesn't mind killing a few hours on the phone with whoever happens to call.

My general rule of thumb is this: If you call to ask a girl out three times and she rejects you every time, move on to a different girl. Three strikes and she's out. Obviously she doesn't like you very much if she keeps making excuses and blowing you off or cancelling your dates. A lot of girls like to use the excuse, "I've just been so busy lately!" The bottom line is this: people make time for the things that are important to them. If a girl likes you, she will make an effort. If she doesn't like you, or is ambivalent, she won't try very hard.

I'm a firm believer in the idea that people should be judged by their actions, not their words. A girl can make you all the promises in the world over the phone, but when push comes to shove, if she's not willing to act on them, those promises are worthless.

This brings up another point about phone behavior: specifically, how many messages should you leave on a girl's answering machine?

I say if you call a girl for the first time and you get her answering machine, leave one message. Wait a day or so. Even with techology as advanced as it is, there is always the possibility that she didn't get the message. Then call and leave one more message. Any more than that is overkill. If she doesn't return your call after the second message, forget about her.

If you leave more than two messages, you're starting to get pathetic. The more messages you leave, the more desperate it makes you seem. This book is not called *The Stalker's Guide to Dating*. And don't keep calling and hanging up when you get her answering machine. She knows it's you. You're not fooling anyone. If you're going to hang up, do it before the answering machine clicks on. At least that way, she doesn't know anyone has called, and she can't star-69 you.

Sometimes it's just better to swallow your pride and cut your losses. Even the best fisherman in the world doesn't catch every fish that pulls on his line. Sometimes you just have to cut that fish loose and move on.

The first time you call a girl is a very intense experience for a Shy Guy. Often you will practice dialing and rehearse the conversation a few times. Even the greeting you use may be rehearsed a few dozen times. I can remember taking several hours—in some cases, days—psyching myself up to call a girl for the first time. And the funny thing is, calling a girl is really not that big of a deal. These days, I just pick up the phone and dial, as casually as if I were calling a friend or a family member.

The greatest fear of most Shy Guys is that once you've called a girl, your secret is out: she knows you like her. You've opened yourself up for potential rejection. There can be no turning back. Well, all that fear and psyching up and rehearsing is unnecessary. Most girls enjoy talking on the phone, and even if she chooses to reject you, she'll probably let you down easy. And if she doesn't want to talk to you, that will be one short phone call, I assure you.

Over the years, girls have developed techniques of rejecting guys that are so painless, it may be days before you realize you've even been rejected. So, go ahead, make that call. Rehearse it a few times if you have to. Practice dialing, if you feel you must. I know one Shy Guy who actually felt the need to write down possible topics of conversation for his first phone call with a new girl.

But by all means, dial the seven digits. Because until you do, you won't be able to stop thinking about it. You'll feel much better afterward.

There are two other types of phone calls I want to mention. One is the Cold Call. You've heard of the expression "cold-cocked" before? It refers to a sudden punch, that comes from out of nowhere and knocks you unconscious.

The Cold Call is based on the same concept. It involves getting a girl's number without her knowledge, either by looking it up in the phone book or getting it through a friend, and then making the call.

The Cold Call is usually a big waste of time. I cannot recommend it, especially for a Shy Guy. If you think it's hard calling a girl who's given you her number, try calling one who who has no idea who you are! Believe me, there's nothing more degrading than calling a girl and having to explain where you met her because she doesn't remember. This is an experience so crushing, so devastating, it can cause a Shy Guy to retreat into his shell permanently.

The final type of call I want to mention is the Out of the Blue Call. This is when there's a girl you may have dated once or twice, or gone to school with, or lived next door to, whom you haven't seen for a while, and you call her out of the blue to ask her out.

Timing is everything with this type of call. Sometimes you get lucky. She may have just broken up with her boyfriend. She may have just returned to the area after having been away for a while. Who knows? She just may be interested in seeing you again. Sometimes a girl needs to date a few jerks before she realizes the perfect guy was living right next door to her the whole time. So it's worth a shot.

One last thing you need to know. If any girl ever tells you she "lost your number," that means she doesn't ever want to see you again. No one ever really loses anyone's number. Trust me on this one. If you like someone, you don't lose their number. It's that simple.

Oh, that reminds me. When a girl gives you her number, I strongly recommend copying it down on another piece of paper when you get home. Having two copies of a girl's number ensures that you will never lose it. It is easy to misplace a crumpled cocktail napkin, so you're better off keeping a permanent listing of important phone numbers. A Rolodex, a home computer, a portable database—any of these will do. It's hard enough for a Shy Guy to get a girl's phone number in the first place. You don't want to risk losing it once you finally get it!

Chapter Six

The First Date

I've spent most of this book trying to get you to ask out a girl. For a Shy Guy this is such a tremendous obstacle, I felt it needed a lot of attention. To most Shy Guys, simply admitting to a girl that they like her is such a major effort, that it can take months—even years—to reach this stage.

But now it's time to move past that. Let's assume you've heeded some of my suggestions and put some of my techniques into practice. You've asked a girl out, and she's said yes. Now it's time for your first date.

Ah, the First Date—the most awkward of all dates. So many bad memories. So many missed opportunities. So many unexpected surprises.

The First Date is the most feared, the most dreaded, the most anxiously awaited date there is. How many of us have lost sleep fretting over that First Date, wishing we could somehow skip it and get right on to the Second Date. How many times have we planned out the whole evening with the precision of a military maneuver, only to watch all our carefully laid plans fall apart from the start?

There is so much tension on a First Date. So much nervous energy. Will you do and say the right things? Will you look cool? Will she think you're a loser? Will you run out of things to talk about? What if you say the wrong thing and she gets offended, and she wants to end the date before it's time? There are so many things that can go wrong, so many variables. A First Date is definitely not for the faint of heart.

I have survived more than a few First Dates, and come out no worse for wear. They are really not that bad and they can be fun. Even if you and your girl do not hit it off, at least you get a good dinner out of it, and you get to check out a movie or concert.

At best, you make a connection with a nice girl and find that she's just as interested in you as you are in her. Generally, you can tell when a date is going well. If you do something really wrong, usually you're aware of it.

I know one guy who, while on a First Date, picked at a shaving cut and found himself unable to stop the bleeding for the rest of the night. On these occasions, all you can do is throw up your hands and say, "Oh well," and hope to do better with the next girl. A bad date may seem like a pretty serious thing today, but you'll be laughing about it years from now.

Girls tend to like a guy who takes charge, so it's usually up to you to suggest a place to go for a first date. The last thing a girl wants to hear is, "I dunno. What do *you* wanna do?" That may be fine when you're hanging out with your buddies in the parking lot at the 7-Eleven, but it does not impress girls. The last thing a girl wants is to go out with a guy who's wishy-washy.

Your best bet for a first date is to choose a moderately-priced restaurant someplace where you feel comfortable. Any T.G.I. Friday's or Bennigan's–type place is usually a good start. If you know the girl is into some sort of exotic food, like sushi, that works fine, too. If there is a band in town that you both want to see, and the tickets are not too expensive, this is another option.

One good idea is to meet a girl for coffee or cocktails on the first date, and then, if it is going well, suggest that the two of you move on to dinner. This way, if things are going poorly, you can just end the date, and you have been spared the cost of a meal.

It's really up to you to determine which method you are most comfortable with. If you really like the girl (and you are really hungry), go for the dinner. If you are low on cash, or are not really sure how you feel about her, go for the coffee or cocktails meeting. Many girls prefer to go to lunch on the first date, as opposed to dinner, because they feel safer. They figure there is less likelihood of your making a move on her in the daytime. Lunch tends to be a shorter meal, and cheaper, than dinner, too. And there is not the automatic assumption that the date will continue beyond the meal, as there might be with a nighttime date.

The worst thing about any First Date is meeting the girl's parents. Parents always want to sit down and talk with you. They always seem genuinely excited to have a new visitor in their home. (I often hit it off better with the parents than I do with the girls I date. Go figure!) The best advice I can give here is that when the girl's parents ask you what your intentions are for the evening, don't say, "I plan on having sex with your daughter!" Your best bet is to play it safe. Try to present yourself as a clean-cut, harmless, asexual guy. (Shy Guys are usually pretty good at this.) Meeting a girl's siblings or roommates is no picnic, either. That's why my preference is to date friendless orphans with no brothers or sisters. Sadly, girls like that are tough to find.

The best you can hope for is to find a girl who's new in town and miles away from everyone she knows. This is why college is such a great place to meet girls. Girls often leave their friends and families thousands of miles behind when they go to college. You may be the only guy she knows in the whole state.

After you and your date have finished dinner, ask her if she would like to go to the movies or rent a video. If she is willing to rent a video, it means she is willing to spend sometime alone on a couch in a dark room with you, so it probably means she likes you. If she agrees to the VCR Date, you will probably have a little smooching session with her after the movie. If she chooses to go to a movie theater instead, keep your hands to yourself. She may not feel that comfortable around you yet; she may not even be that attracted to you.

The VCR Date has grown increasingly popular in recent years. It is an inexpensive and fun way for a couple to spend an evening. Instead of spending fifteen, twenty bucks in a theater, the VCR Date can run you as low as two or three dollars, and you have a much wider selection of movies to choose from.

Heck, if you are like most Shy Guys, you probably have a huge collection of videos to choose from at your house, so that saves you a trip to the video store. Not to mention the fact that taking a girl back to your place to watch a video gives you all-important Home Court Advantage. By agreeing to enter your castle to watch the video, a girl has entered into a nonverbal contract with you to engage in a little frisky business. No words need be said. It is simply understood. So it is written, so it shall be done. Rare indeed is the girl who agrees to the VCR Date with no intention of engaging in a smooching session.

Back when I used to date pretty heavily, I joined a mail-order video club through which I bought a whole bunch of videos which I call the Crowd Pleaser Collection. These were popular, inoffensive movies that were guaranteed to provide an entertaining night. I bought a cross-section of recent hits—action films, comedies, romance, horror. You can also pick up used videos pretty cheap at your local video store.

If you plan to have a girl over to watch a video, it is probably a good idea to have some kind of liquor in the house—beer, wine, wine coolers, whatever she is into. (This is assuming you are both over twenty-one, of course!) It makes you seem classy, even if she chooses not to take you up on your offer.

For God's sake, make sure you have some privacy. This may be a bit tricky if you live at home, but if you live with roommates, make sure they are out of the house when you and your little lady arrive. The last thing you need is some clueless roommate sitting on the couch with you when you and your girl are trying to get romantic. Most parents are usually pretty accommodating about giving you and your date a little breathing room, but it can be a little awkward trying to put the moves on a girl if her mom is in the next room.

Try to go to the house that will have the least amount of interference. If you know your home is going to be free of distractions, try to convince her to go there. If you have to borrow a friend's apartment, go for it.

I strongly recommend turning off the lights when you watch your video. It increases the possibility of something happening in the petting department. Make sure you sit on the side of the couch you are most comfortable with. As a righty, I prefer to sit on a girl's left side. If a girl tries to sit in my preferred spot, I politely ask her to move by saying, "That's my seat!"

If you have to get up and go to the bathroom, by all means, get up and go. She'll be fine on her own for a few minutes. But make sure you don't leave anything incriminating behind for her to discover, such as your address book, your porno mag collection, or those naked pictures you took of your last girlfriend.

And whatever you do, if you bring home a date and the little red light on your answering machine is blinking, *do not*, under any circumstances, play your messages. For all you know, it might be another girl. Or it might be one of your buddies asking, "Hey, dude, how did your date go? Did you score?" Whatever the message is, it can wait until after she's gone.

You may choose to forego the after-dinner movie route entirely, instead opting to go for coffee, dessert, cocktails, or a quiet little jazz club around the corner. Whatever you're into. Another good first date is a sporting event. But, again, make sure the tickets are reasonably priced.

You've seen enough TV to know what a first date is supposed to look like. But for the sake of you novices, I've compiled a handy list of Dos and Don'ts for a First Date.

DO . . . take her out to dinner at a nice restaurant. (No McDonald's!) Bring enough money to pay for the two of you, but if she offers to pay half, that's cool. A really classy girl will always at least offer to pay for her share. Whether or not you choose to accept her offer depends on your financial situation and how badly you are trying to impress her. If you are exceptionally shy, take her to a movie so you don't have to talk to her for two hours, and you'll have something to talk about afterwards.

DO NOT . . . try to make a move on her in the movie theater. Richie Cunningham may get a lot of action this way, but this is real life. She'll respect you a lot more if you just watch the movie. If you think she has a strong attraction to you, you may want to slip your arm around her, or run your fingers through her hair a little, but leave it at that. The first date is just the warmup. The second date is when you want to start getting into the physical stuff, because if she's dating you a second time, that usually means she likes you.

DON'T . . . take her to a nudie bar, as Dustin Hoffman with Katharine Ross in *The Graduate*. No matter how much you may enjoy the Booby Trap, take my word for it, she's not going to appreciate it as much as you do. Also, do not take her to a porno movie, as Robert De Niro did with Cybill Shepherd on their first date in *Taxi Driver*. Likewise, I'd stray away from even suggesting kinky "swingers" clubs until you know her *really* well.

DO . . . pick her up on time. Do not be late. I can't stress this one enough! If she lives in an area you're not familiar with, you may want to practice driving to her house. Try to find it during the daytime, so you know you'll be able to find it at night. Just make sure she doesn't see you.

DON'T . . . park outside her house a few hours before the date and wait for her. I keep telling you, you've got to stop thinking like a stalker.

DO . . . dress nice. Girls appreciate a guy who is a sharp dresser. As ZZ Top once said, "Every girl's crazy 'bout a sharp dressed man!" Don't show up in jeans and a t-shirt, unless you're taking her to a rodeo. Make sure you bathe before your date. Use soap and shampoo. Comb your hair. I'm not your mother. I shouldn't have to tell you these things!

DON'T . . . slap on so much cologne that you smell like your swingin' Uncle Louie with the funky Hawaiian shirt.

DO . . . clean your room or apartment before you go out, just in case.

DO . . . buy some fresh condoms, just in case. The one that's been in your wallet since you were thirteen just won't cut it. As long as you're in the drug store, pick up some breath mints or sugarless gum (whichever you prefer). These will come in handy later on, as I'll explain in the chapter on "How to Score."

DO . . . tell your date how nice she looks—even if you don't think she looks that great. Remember what I said earlier: every girl likes a compliment.

DON'T . . . show more interest in the waitress than you do in her. Once while on a first date, a friend of mine remarked that the waitress had great legs. I swear, this really happened! Needless to say, the date ended badly. Save that kind of talk for the locker room. No matter how attractive the waitress may be, do not flirt with her!

DON'T . . . ask your date about her dating history. Don't ask her about past boyfriends. All of this stuff will come out in time as you get to know her. Some girls like to spend a whole date talking about their other boyfriends. Boring! Do whatever you can to change the topic.

DON'T . . . reveal too much about your dating history, especially if you haven't dated very much. People will often assume you have a life unless you prove otherwise. If you reveal you haven't had many girlfriends, she may think there's something wrong with you. You don't want to give away too much information on the first date. By being a little secretive, you build up a little mystery, and this makes her want to get to know you better. When information comes out slowly and gradually, she will be a lot more intrigued by you, and she will begin to wonder what other interesting things there are about you that she doesn't know.

DON'T . . . expect to get laid on the first date. Most girls don't go for that sort of thing, unless you're dating the town slut. Usually the first date is a way of gauging how well you like each other. It'll be worth waiting for. Don't blow your chances by being overanxious.

DON'T . . . tell her you love her. Hey, pal, it's only your first date! I don't care how well you know her, you don't want to scare her away.

DON'T . . . talk too much about your bizarre hobbies. You may have some great theories about UFO conspiracies, but save them for when she knows you better.

DON'T . . . tell any off-color jokes. She may not appreciate them. Likewise, don't use any foul language, unless you're dating a lady trucker.

DON'T . . . invite any of your friends to join you on the date. Typically, when a Shy Guy first asks a girl out on a date, he will say something like, "Me and all my friends are going to the movies. Why don't you come with us?" A Shy Guy feels safe using this line because he's not really asking the girl out on a date—it's more like a group activity. This way, if the girl says no, she's not really rejecting the Shy Guy; she's rejecting the whole group, and so the pain is lessened.

Forget about this approach. The only way to really show a girl you like her is to take her out one on one. If you invite her along with all your friends, she may think you just see her as another friend. If you keep inviting her to join you on group activities, you'll probably only end up frustrating yourself.

Trust me on this one. Even bringing one other friend with you on a date changes the whole dynamic of the evening. I'm a big believer in making it very clear to the girl that you want to have a *date* with her—not a get-together, not a social gathering with a bunch of friends, not a meeting, not a friendly night out, but a *date*—a genuine, "I'll pick you up at eight and it ends in a kiss" date!

Whatever you do, don't tell her, "You can bring some of your friends along, if you want." This is not what you want. You want to spend some quality time with the girl alone, so you can find out if you really like each other. Throwing any other person into the mix reduces your date to a social gathering.

Even worse, what if you invite one of your buddies along and your date likes your friend better? What if your friend just won't shut up and monopolizes the conversation? Now see what you've done? You've just shot yourself in the foot! You may have blown any chance you had with this girl, all because you were too scared to face her alone.

You're better off leaving your friends at home. You're a big boy now. Your friends have always been there for you, but now it's time to go off on your own. Your friends will still be there for you after the date is over.

DON'T . . . talk about any of your freaky sexual fantasies or perversions. Save that stuff for *much later* on in the relationship.

DO . . . try to keep the conversation light and fun. Try to stay away from serious topics like death, politics, and religion.

DON'T . . . ask her any really personal questions.

DON'T . . . admit to too many of your flaws right off the bat. If you start off by telling her, "Well, I'm not very good with money; I spend everything I've got, and I love to gamble; I owe so much money to so many people," you'll never see this girl again.

DON'T . . . get in an argument with her. Remember, the first date is really just a chance for you two to get to know each other better, to see if you're compatible. You can save the arguments for after you get married.

DON'T . . . bring her a bouquet of flowers and a box of candy, unless you want to show her you're hopelessly old-fashioned. That kind of stuff went out of style in your grandfather's day. I'd stay away from expensive jewelry, too.

DON'T . . . spend too much money on a first date. I once had a friend who took a girl out to a ritzy Manhattan restaurant on the first date, followed by dancing at the Palladium, where it costs fifteen bucks a head to get in, and drinks are seven bucks each. Total cost for the night: about two hundred dollars! My friend never saw the girl again after that, though it was a night he will never forget. If you can afford this kind of night, fine, but otherwise, I'd say forty dollars is about the highest you want to go on a first date.

DO . . . end the date by telling her, "I had a great time tonight. I'll definitely call you again." Even if you don't mean it, it still sounds nice.

DO . . . tell all your friends about the date. Hey, that's half the fun of dating. Besides, she's gonna tell all her friends about it! You can leave out the sex parts, though. If you really like a girl, you don't want to air the details of your sex life all over town.

DO . . . call her again, but only if you like her. Sometimes you find the magic just isn't there. Sometimes you discover you just don't like her as much as you thought you would. That's okay. It happens. There's no law that says every boy and girl who go out on one date must fall for each other.

In the event that you find she's not what you expected, you're not obligated to call her again, even if you said you would. She'll get the hint. I've had several experiences where a girl really liked me after one date, but I just didn't feel any kind of connection with her. In these instances, I find it best just to move on. Just because you've dated someone one time does not mean you have any kind of obligation to her. The girl's feelings may be a little hurt, but she'll get over it. Better to let her go than to lead her on. If you have no real interest in a girl, pursuing her is only wasting her time and yours.

Likewise, if she blows you off after one date, forget about her. It's not the end of the world. According to a statistic that I just made up, only 50 percent of all first dates lead to a second date.

If you're one of the lucky ones who gets it right the first time, consider yourself fortunate. Most of us have endured one nightmarish first date after another. In a perfect world, you would only have to endure one first date, and that would be with the girl you end up marrying.

Wouldn't it be great if your first First Date could be your last?

The Ten Best Date Movies

In order to make things a little easier for you, I'm going to suggest ten movies on video that are always a good way to spend a first date. These movies are mostly lighthearted, and decidely non-controversial. You don't want to bring your date down with a depressing movie, or get her all riled up over some controversial issue. For instance, the Jodie Foster flick, *The Accused*, where she gets raped on a pool table, is not a good date movie. I also would not recommend the Tina Turner biography, *What's Love Got to Do With It*, in which Tina is battered repeatedly by her husband, Ike.

As a general rule, you want to see a love story on a date. But, being a guy, you don't want to see something exceptionally sappy. You need to find a good balance between what a guy wants and what a girl wants. That's why a flick like *Jerry Maguire* is an ideal choice. It's got sports stuff for the guys, and mushy romance stuff for the girls.

Here then, is my suggested list of good date movies.

An Officer and a Gentleman (1982): My personal all-time favorite romantic movie. Girls are captivated by its tale of a selfish man who learns to care about others. It's also got a catchy theme song, "Up Where We Belong" by Joe Cocker and Jennifer Warnes! Richard Gere gives the best performance of his career, and Debra Winger has never looked better. In my experience, there is no better movie for getting women in the mood for love! And if you own a white sailor suit, it can only increase your chances of scoring.

Ghost (1990): Based on the amount of money this block-buster made when it first came out, it's got to be one of the most beloved love stories of our generation. Girls seemed to be enchanted by its story of a love that would not die. It has a little humor, thanks to Whoopi Goldberg, a little suspense, and a very photogenic lead couple in Demi Moore and Patrick Swayze. By the time it's over, your date will be crying her eyes out.

(If you're really looking to score some points with a girl, rent *Somewhere in Time*, the 1980 Christopher Reeve/Jane Seymour flick that many gals consider to be the most romantic movie of all time. Guys hate it, though, so be prepared to be bored.)

GREASE (1978): This movie is a love story, but it's also a comedy, and a very funny one at that. It is one of the most entertaining movies of all time. Everyone loves the music from *Grease*, and John Travolta and Olivia Newton-John make a great couple. This movie was an essential part of growing up for every member of Generation X; it holds a lot of nostalgia for people who saw it when it first came out back in the seventies.

THE AMERICAN PRESIDENT (1995): Every girl fantasizes about dating the president of the United States. Since all the presidents we've had for the past few decades have been happily married (yeah, right), it has not been possible for any of these fantasies to come true. Critic Leonard Maltin calls this flick, "the ultimate wish-fulfillment movie, with a president who's handsome, funny, decisive, forthright, and honest." By the time you're done watching it, you'll have your date singing "Hail to the Chief!"

SILENCE OF THE LAMBS (1991): Back in the days when I used to date heavily, just about every girl who came over my house chose to watch *The Silence of the Lambs*. I got so sick of seeing that movie, I doubt I could ever watch it again. It seems to be a very popular choice among girls. Perhaps one reason is because it has Jodie Foster in the lead. It's a known fact that the most successful horror movies have strong female leads. Look at all of the *Nightmare on Elm Street* movies and most of the *Friday the Thirteenth* flicks. Girls generally don't like to watch horror flicks unless they have strong female leads. It is sometimes good to watch a scary movie on a date, because the girl may get frightened and want to hold your hand, or huddle close to you, or whatever.

Another mega-popular horror movie is *Scream* (1996), which offers every girl that ultimate wish-fulfillment fantasy of her boyfriend turning out to be a deranged serial killer. To be honest, I don't understand why girls love this mediocre movie so much, but love it they do. Apparently a lot of young ladies have some real trust issues to work out with their boyfriends.

When Harry Met Sally . . . (1989): A very funny, insightful movie about relationships. This movie is equally fun for guys and gals. Billy Crystal and Meg Ryan make a great couple. If you like this one, you may also like *Sleepless in Seattle* (1991), from the same writer (Nora Ephron). I hated *Sleepless*, but it was incredibly popular, so obviously I'm in the minority here. The bottom line is that *Sleepless* is a good date movie, even though it is your typical lightweight, predictable, sappy Hollywood romance.

. . . About Last Night (1986): A fun movie starring Rob Lowe and Demi Moore as a young couple who make those first tentative steps toward commitment when they move in together. This is a fairly realistic movie about people finding out all those little things about each other that make relationships interesting. Jim Belushi has a very funny role as Rob's raunchy pal who always advises him to behave like a typical insensitive guy. The only thing I don't like in this flick is the ending, where Rob Lowe's character gets a little too pathetic. Other than that, *. . . About Last Night* is a very entertaining movie about a couple you can really root for.

INDECENT PROPOSAL (1991): This Demi Moore/Robert Redford flick created a minicontroversy as couples all across America argued over whether they would let their partner sleep with someone else for a million dollars. This is the type of "controversy" that could only come out of Hollywood. Since it could never happen in real life, the question is rather irrelevent, isn't it? It's like asking, if your wife turned into a werewolf, would you still love her? Still, lotsa people enjoyed this dopey flick. At any rate, Demi Moore looked real good in the black dress, and there is a sex scene on a bed filled with money, which are probably the only memorable images to come out of the movie.

BRAVEHEART (1994): Girls go crazy over the romanticism displayed by Mel Gibson in this flick, who is inspired by the death of his wife to set his country free! Ol' Braveheart really would do anything for love. (Chicks are suckers for old-fashioned, medieval-type movies, like *Willow*, *Robin Hood: Prince of Thieves*, etc.) It's also got lots of action for the guys. This is a long one, so you'd better start it early. Since *Braveheart* clocks in at nearly three hours, you'd better start it by 9:00 if you plan on having a smooching session afterward. Otherwise, you'll be too pooped to pucker up.

THE BODYGUARD (1992): This Kevin Costner/Whitney Houston flick scored big at the box office—but does anyone really buy these two as lovers? I didn't believe it for a minute. Still, it was an entertaining yarn. It's a love story where the woman loves herself more than she loves anyone else. (Maybe she should have sung "I Will Always Love Me.") Still, the movie has a decent mystery storyline, and an excellent soundtrack.

If your date has a taste for danger, you may want to rent an erotic thriller together. Girls love to see movies in the "women in jeopardy" genre, which is why all those TV movies are so popular, where every week another member of the cast of *Melrose Place* or *Beverly Hills 90210* gets in trouble. Among the better theatrical flicks in this category are: *Fatal Attraction, Sleeping With the Enemy, Unlawful Entry, The Hand That Rocks the Cradle*, and *Basic Instinct*.

Just be careful if you rent one of these. Strange as it may seem, *Fatal Attraction* is not always a great first date movie. Make sure the girl has a good sense of humor.

If you've already seen all of the above movies, and can't seem to find anything else, I have another rule of thumb: when in doubt, go with *Forrest Gump*. It won the Academy Award for Best Picture of 1994, and everyone seems to love this fable about a simple-minded man who stumbles his way through some of the most significant events in U.S. history. *Gump* features at its heart a love story between Forrest and his girl Jenny, and it even has a main character die of AIDS at the end. If there's one thing girls love, it's a movie in which somebody gets sick and dies. (*Terms of Endearment, Dying Young, Steel Magnolias*, etc.) Girls love to cry over a movie. This movie gives them that opportunity.

As for movies to avoid, I suppose it goes without saying you should stay away from porno flicks. Many couples like to use X-rated movies to spice up their love lives, but save that for later in the relationship. Of course, if your date wanders into the porno room at the video store by herself and seems excited, then it's a different story!

Likewise, as much as you may enjoy bloody gorefests like *Evil Dead II*, you'd better check with your date first and see if she's into that kind of thing.

Now, at this point, some of you may be saying, "Okay, enough about movies already! What if she doesn't like movies? What do we do then, hotshot?" Well, first of all, let me say I'm not sure I like your attitude. But I'll try to help you anyway.

Here now is my list of

Top Ten Things to Do on a Date If She Doesn't Like Movies

1) Meet in the park on a sunny day and go for a walk; you may wish to bring a picnic basket and a Frisbee.

2) Go to a comedy club.

3) Go to a carnival or county fair.

4) If the girl is adventurous, go to an arcade where they have virtual reality games.

5) Go horseback riding.

6) Go to a play.

7) Go to a casino or racetrack, if there is one nearby.

8) Go to one of those Medieval Times fairs, where everyone dresses up like knights and has jousts with each other. Remember what I told you—chicks love those medieval kinds of things! Some girls are also into Renaissance Festivals.

9) Go to one of those cybercafes where you and your date can have fun going online and exploring different web sites.

10) You can't go wrong with a jazz club.

I have one friend who takes his dates bird-watching. Another friend recommends poetry readings. A third suggests attending church functions. If your date is into cars, you may want to try an auto show. Others may enjoy sailing. You may want to try one of those murder-mystery dinner theater deals. Spend a day at the beach. Go to a pool hall. Go to the zoo, a museum, an aquarium. Go Rollerblading, skiing, hang gliding, skydiving. See how creative you can be. The sky really is the limit.

I'm fortunate to live in South Florida—the festival capital of North America. It seems like every weekend, there is another festival going on, whether it be a wine festival, a seafood festival, or an arts and crafts show. They're always closing off the streets for some festival or another. When you live in a place that has a warm climate all year round, it only increases the number of places you can take a date.

But even if you don't live someplace that's warm all the time, there is still plenty of stuff to do indoors. When I lived in the New York area, I used to send away for tickets to local TV shows and take girls to see tapings of *Late Night with David Letterman* and *Saturday Night Live*. These tickets are free, so it was a cheap date, although there is a long wait for the tickets—sometimes up to a year or more.

There really is no limit to the amount of things you can do on a date. It all depends on what you are both into. If the two of you are really interested in getting together, you can come up with something. The main thing is that you not be afraid to ask her what she enjoys. You may be pleasantly surprised to learn the two of you have more in common than you thought.

Chapter Seven

Making Out!

How do you score with a girl? This is a good question, one that many Shy Guys face. Even if you survive the emotional turmoil of asking a girl out, you still have to deal with the even more agonizing prospect of trying to put the moves on her. This is where most Shy Guys really drop the ball. The average Shy Guy is too timid to put the moves on a girl on a first date. Or the second. Or the third. After a while, the girl starts to wonder if you are gay.

Better to make the effort and have her know you're straight than to make like a boy scout and leave her wondering. As a general rule, when it comes to first dates, I like to use what I call the Potsie Scale. The way it works is this: on the old TV show *Happy Days*, Richie and Potsie used to take girls to the movies and make out with them on the first date. Usually this was done in the movie theater or in a jalopy by the lake. Back then, they called it "watching the submarine races!"

These days, we live in more sophisticated times, and you don't see a heck of a lot of people over the age of fifteen making out at the movies any more. Besides, that's kind of aggressive for a first date, don't you think?

No, you're better off waiting until the movie is over, and then putting your moves on her on her doorstep when you say goodnight. My basic feeling is this: Potsie was at least getting to first base on his dates, and he was a nerd! If I can't at least get to first base with a girl on the first date, that means I'm doing worse than Potsie! That puts me below a nerd! And you don't want to be considered a subnerd now, do you?

So unless you want Potsie Webber to have a better social life than you, you'd better at least offer to walk her to her door and try for a kiss. There is probably no more awkward moment in your life than when you are standing with a girl on her doorstep, struggling for conversation, afraid to kiss her because you're not sure how she will respond. Most Shy Guys just stand there like idiots, as their date shrugs her shoulders, says "goodnight," and closes the door, all the while wondering why you didn't kiss her. Generally, she's not going to make the first move, so if you don't act in this situation, you get nothing. That means the whole date was for nothing, and you're going to have to go through this again next time. With most guys, the entire first date is focused on: how far am I going to get on her doorstep? If you get nothing, you've just wasted an entire night.

Some guys are so shy, they feel they must ask for the kiss. Generally, you shouldn't have to ask for it. Just walk her up to the door, say goodnight, and dive right in. Look her in the eye. Does she look like she wants you to kiss her, or is she slamming the door in your face? If she closes the door on you, that's usually a good indication she doesn't want to kiss you! But if she lingers for a few minutes at the door and her head starts moving toward yours, she's probably up for some smooching.

If she opens her mouth for the kiss, she probably wants you

to stick your tongue down her throat. A lot of Shy Guys get real timid when it comes to French kissing. They're afraid it's too bold. Well, a lot of girls really enjoy French kissing, so it's in your best interests to probe around her mouth a little and see if she's up for it. If she gives you the close-mouthed kiss, or the peck on the cheek, obviously she doesn't want you tonguing her. Again, if a girl does not want your tongue in her mouth, she will let you know real quick!

One thing I'd like to stress here is that most girls really love kissing. I mean, they love it! They seem to get far more pleasure out of it than men do. Girls could just kiss their boyfriends for hours, and never feel they were missing out on anything. Us guys tend to need a little more stimulation than that. Eventually, most guys reach an age where kissing alone just doesn't do it for them. Within a few minutes after kissing begins, a guy's hands will start wandering. Girls are usually quick to grab those hands and hold them to prevent further groping.

It may be hard for guys to accept, much less understand, but just because a girl enjoys kissing you does not mean she wants to do anything else with you—especially on her front porch, where all the neighbors can watch.

If a girl invites you into her house to "watch TV," well, that's a different story. Now, at least, there's the possibility she may be interested in doing something beyond just kissing. Let me paint a scenario for you. The two of you are alone in her apartment. The lights are dimmed. Only the TV is on. You're sitting together on the couch. Maybe she has poured a couple of glasses of wine. Chances are, she's waiting for you to make your move. Most girls don't want to appear too eager, so they generally won't make the first move. She's done her part by inviting you in and setting the scene—I'm afraid that the rest is up to you.

The question is, how do you do it? Believe it or not, there are Shy Guys who are so paralyzed by fear of rejection, they would actually sit there for a few hours watching TV and then leave, without even trying for a kiss! The sad fact is that many guys lack either the confidence or the know-how to make a move in this situation.

I once had a fellow Shy Guy present me with this very dilemma: "Okay—you're on a couch with a girl. You're watching TV. How do you go from 'We're watching TV' to 'We're making out?' "

Over the years, I've developed a system of figuring out how to accomplish this most difficult of tasks. It is a method so surefire, even Beavis and Butthead could use it to score. (Well, maybe not Beavis.)

You take a girl out to dinner or a movie. Afterwards, you invite her back to your place to "watch some TV." Or, if you have something really interesting at your place, like an antique car collection, or a pet lizard, invite her back to your place to see it. The more unique and obscure the item, the greater will be her desire to see it. If you have a creative side, invite her back to your place to see your sketches, paintings, poems, whatever. If you are a halfway-talented filmmaker, offer her to show her one of your short films. (No porno! You don't want to do anything to scare her off so soon.)

If the girl agrees to come with you back to your place, it generally means she has some attraction to you. Most girls know what a guy means when he says, "Come back to my place."

One thing you may wish to do is set the mood. Dim the lights, if possible. Light some candles, particularly scented ones. Girls love scented candles! You will also want to make sure your breath is fresh. As noted earlier, breath mints or gum will help with this. Just make sure you spit out your gum before the festivities begin, because some girls get annoyed to find you chewing during a makeout session. It's also important that you brush your tongue after every meal. Not only does this eliminate germs, but it also helps prevent bad breath! It would be a shame to lose a girl just because you had gingivitis!

One good rule of thumb is to offer a piece of gum to your date. If she accepts, it usually means she is interested in smooching. And if *she* offers *you* a piece of gum, that probably means she's warm for your form. That's another one of those little clues you have to pay attention to.

Instead of TV, you may wish to listen to romantic music. To me, the best makeout music of all time is Sade's *Love Deluxe* album, but any Sade album will do. As cliched as it is, you may also want to try a classical piece, like Ravel's "Bolero." This is the music Dudley Moore played when he made it with Bo Derek in the movie *10*. It has since become perhaps the corniest makeout music ever, but try it yourself sometime—it really works!

Once you and the girl are alone on the couch, you have to assume that she likes you. After all, she could have gone home if all she really wanted to do was watch TV.

If she likes you, she probably won't mind if you put your arm around her. (One way to do this is with the old fake yawn. This is a dating trick that dates back to the Stone Age. In fact, it is rumored that it's how Fred Flintstone bagged Wilma.) I've rented videos with girls where I spent the entire two hours agonizing over whether I should put my arm around her or not. Before you know it, you're watching the end credits roll, and you've just wasted another evening. However you choose to do it, try to get your arm around her as early in the evening as possible. The longer you wait, the more you will think about it, and the harder it will be to actually do.

If she lets you put your arm around her, it probably means she wants you to kiss her. Start with a few gentle kisses and see how she responds. If she pulls away, she may not be interested. But keep trying anyway. It could be she just doesn't want to appear "easy." Be persistent, but if she gives you a firm "No!" back off.

If she lets you kiss her mouth, go for the neck and ears. The ear is one of the most erogenous zones women have. Blow in it or stick your tongue in it, and you'll be amazed by the reactions it produces.

If a girl lets you kiss her, she probably won't mind if you feel her breast. Start out by going over her blouse. If she has no problem with that, try going under. If she lets you touch her breast, she'll probably let you touch her butt.

If she lets you touch her butt, she may, I repeat, *may*, let you slide your hand down her panties. This is why we guys like girls who wear dresses or skirts—the shorter, the better! It's much easier to reach into a girl's panties when she is wearing a dress or skirt. Blue jeans are very tough to get into. That takes a lot of work. And if a girl definitely wants to keep you out of her privates, she wears one of those bodysuits, which are impossible for you to pull off. It's kind of her insurance that you won't go too far.

One thing you may want to try here is to offer her a back rub, or see if she's willing to give you one. If your date complains of a sore neck, reach over and start massaging it for her. No girl in the world will resist a back rub if she's in the mood for one. I would say some of the greatest sexual encounters of all time started with an innocent back rub. There's just something about hands rubbing bodies that puts people in the mood for love!

Start by rubbing her back and neck, then work your way down to her butt. Try to reach around front to massage her breasts. If nothing else, at least you can cop a couple of cheap feels. If she lets you touch her private parts, tell her the massage will be better if she removes her shirt. She just may be willing. From there, you're just a few steps away from scoring. You may even want to purchase some massage oil to enhance the experience.

You can purchase massage lotion at any bath and body shop at your local mall.

After massaging your girl, see if she is willing to massage you in return. After you are both oiled up, it can lead to a superslippery lovemaking session. Or as a buddy of mine once put it, "I like to grease my girl up like a pig before I do her!"

Even if you have a girl on your couch and you are on her like an octopus, there are no guarantees that you will go all the way. This is why the Baseball Scale of making out was invented. For those of you who weren't paying attention in grade school, the scale goes like this:

First Base: Kissing (with tongue)
Second Base: Breast Fondling (preferably under her bra)
Third Base: You get your fingers in her panties
Home Run: Sex (though I'm sure you could figure that one out for yourself)

Third base can be the most difficult base of all. Many is the man who has been safe at second and thrown out at third. Many girls will hold you comfortably at second. Stealing third can be a real challenge. But it's worth going for, because once you're on third base, a home run is just one base away.

I was going to get a little graphic here and describe what comes next with the whole "Making Out" thing, but my editor has respectfully asked me to keep it clean and I'm honoring her wishes. I would like to point out, though, that different girls have different standards. Some girls just like to kiss. If you even lay one finger on their breast, they will act all shocked and ask you, "What are you doing?!" Some girls act stunned that you would actually try to touch their body. They are mortified that just because they have their tongue down your throat, you thought you could try something a little more physical.

Some girls will let you touch their breasts and butts, but that's it. Some girls will let you put your hand—and *only* your hand—down their panties. Then there are girls who call themselves virgins, who will still perform oral sex on you, and generally do just about everything except penetration. Don't expect any two girls to act the same. It all has to do with how they were raised, what kind of values they grew up with, and how much they like you.

The important thing is to always let the girl dictate what you can and cannot do. If she says you can't touch her someplace, don't touch her there. Sometimes a girl starts off saying you can't do certain things, but then she starts getting turned on, she changes her mind and lets you go to town. So keep trying. You never know when a "no" can turn into a "yes." Ultimately, though, it's her choice.

Try not to shoot your load too soon. If you get too excited, the girl will quickly realize you haven't done this very often. Some girls are turned off when you get too enthusiastic. The best thing to do is to take it slow and easy. Most girls say they like sex slow and gentle. Of course, if the girl turns out to be a sex-crazed she-vixen who digs her nails into your back, you may choose to pick up the pace a little.

If you have any questions about how to make love to a woman, there are plenty of books you can pick up on the subject. This is really more of a "getting over your shyness" book than a "how to make love to a woman" book. But there are plenty of those out there. Just go back to the self-help section of your book store and look around. Try to find one with lots of juicy pictures! I recommend a book called the *Kama Sutra*. It contains photos of every sex position ever conceived of. If you're feeling adventurous, why not get a copy of this book and see how many positions you and your girl can go through in one weekend?

One thing that you may want to do when making love with a

girl is to ask her what she likes her partner to do and, if it's something you have no objection to, do it for her. She will find it a big turn-on that you are willing to please her and she will usually reciprocate. Tell her what you like and she may do it for you. The important thing here is not to be shy! You were brave enough to ask her on a date; don't stop being brave now, just because you both have your clothes off. Shy Guys tend to have very puritanical ideas on love-making—we don't like to talk about it and we don't get very experimental. We just like to do it in the most traditional manner possible. We go for the old Missionary Position whenever possible. But many women like to be on top. Switching positions every now and then can only increase the satisfaction of both partners.

In opening up to your girl and discussing what turns you on, you may find you're willing to please each other in all kinds of different ways. This will increase the pleasure of your lovemaking sessions significantly.

Any time you go on a date, you always want to bring a condom with you, just in case. I can't stress this enough. We live in an age where you can die from sex, so it's foolish to not use any kind of protection. This is an area where Shy Guys often have a problem, because in the heat of the moment, they are too shy to stop and put on a condom. They are afraid that any interruption in the foreplay could kill the mood and the girl might cancel the whole thing. You really don't have to worry about this.

If the girl likes you, she will respect you even more for stopping to get some protection. If she is bothered that you insist on wearing on a condom, she is probably not a girl you want to sleep with anyway. If the girl says you don't need to wear protection, wear it anyway. You don't know where she's been. As the old cliche goes, when you sleep with someone, you're also sleeping with every partner they've ever had.

I once had a girl tell me she couldn't get pregnant. This is a ridiculous argument. Every girl can get pregnant, no matter what they tell you. Avoid the "pull-out" method or the "rhythm" method. Stick to condoms. They are the only form of birth control with a 99 percent rate of effectiveness.

There is nothing wrong with a little consensual sex. It can be a lot of fun, as long as you do it safely. And for God's sake, make sure the girl is old enough. Sex may be a lot of fun, but it's not worth going to jail for.

Oh yeah, if you are the old-fashioned type of guy who wants to wait to have sex until he finds the right girl, or until after he gets married, there is nothing wrong with that. We live in an age where we are bombarded by sexual imagery on TV, the movies, and the radio. It's all around us, and, when combined with peer pressure, some of you may feel pushed into doing something you're not comfortable with.

If a girl comes on to you, and you're just not ready for sex yet, simply tell her you're not that type of guy. And be firm. Let her know that no means no! A Shy Guy can make an easy target for an aggressive female—especially if she pumps you full of liquor!

I have one friend who used to come on to girls all the time, but he never had any luck whatsoever. He stayed a virgin until he got married. He once told me his ultimate dream was to only have one lover his entire life. He got his wish, and you've got to admire that sentiment. In this day and age, it's rare to find somebody who refuses to cave in to media messages and peer pressure to have casual sex. I give my friend a lot of credit for that.

Of course, the fact that he was a lousy pickup artist may have made his choice a little easier!

Chapter Eight

EXTREME DATING (AKA Unconventional Methods)

So far, we've covered some pretty traditional ways of meeting girls. In this chapter, we're going to turn the dating world on its side. We're going to get you to look at some different ways of hooking up—methods that may seem a little radical at first, but in retrospect will seem perfectly logical, even ingenius, when you stop to reflect on them.

Just remember: no approach is too extreme. There is no place you cannot go to meet girls. (Okay, maybe a funeral is a little tasteless, but don't rule it out completely.) The following are but a small sample of different methods of what I like to call Extreme Dating.

THE BEST PLACES TO MEET A GIRL THAT YOU NEVER WOULD HAVE THOUGHT OF

Don't like going to bars? Don't live near a beach? No problem! Here's a list of somewhat more unconventional places where you can pick up babes!

1) A bowling alley: I actually did this once! This works best if the girl is bowling in the next lane with her friends. Maybe you can challenge them to a game, show them some tips, or ask them how the scoring works.
2) The scene of a car accident: I'm not suggesting you crash into anyone, but a little fender bender is a great conversation-starter!
3) On a plane, bus, or train trip: The girl is stuck sitting next to you for a couple of hours, so you'll have her undivided attention. The only way you could get more attention from her is if you kidnapped her! And I wouldn't recommend that route, since while it is true that hostages often wind up falling for their kidnappers, I think you're really pressing your luck with this one. Likewise, I wouldn't advise burning down a girl's house to get her attention, like that kid did to Brooke Shields in *Endless Love*. I mean, come on, people—let's use a little common sense here!
4) In the waiting room at the dentist's office: First make sure she doesn't have gum disease. For that matter, see if the hygienist is cute. You could actually meet a girl while sitting in the dentist's chair. A good line to use here is, "Usually I don't let a girl stick her fingers in my mouth before the first date."
5) In the airport, while waiting for your luggage at the

baggage carousel: You have both just arrived from the same place, so presumably you will have something to talk about. "So, how did you like Monaco? Did you do any gambling?" Etc., etc. Also, while sitting in the airport, waiting to board your flight, you can pick out a girl who is also waiting and strike up a conversation. Since you're both going to the same place, this could save you the hassle of meeting someone when you get there. If she takes an instant liking to you, she may even suggest the two of you sit together on the flight.

6) Waiting in line at the post office, bank, or DMV: Whenever I move to a new area, I like to check out the bank tellers at all the local banks first and then deposit my money at whichever bank has the cutest chicks! However, if you date a bank teller, just remember, there may be a penalty for early withdrawal! Ha ha ha ha ha ha ha ha! I love that joke! (Sorry, I'm just trying to lighten the mood a little here. Or am I losing your "interest"?)
7) While pumping gas: This works best in those states where they have self-service gas stations. You're filling up your gas tank at the pump next to hers. You turn to her and ask, "Do you pump here often?" or something equally clever. You may even offer to pump her gas for her, saying "A pretty lady like you should never have to get her hands dirty."
8) During jury duty: You've got a captive audience! For at least two days, the two of you are stuck in a room together. No matter what kind of trial you end up on, it would be criminal to let an opportunity like this go to waste!

9) At a wedding: As shown by the movie *Prizzi's Honor*, a wedding is a good place to pick up women.
10) On a ski lift.

Going Solo

Stop me if you've heard this one. A bunch of Shy Guys walk into a bar. They see some pretty, single girls. They want to talk to the girls but instead, they talk only to each other. Then the pretty girls leave and the Shy Guys go home alone.

Waiting for the punchline? There is none. This is no joke, I'm afraid. It's a situation that Shy Guys find themselves in every night. Most people tend to hang out with other people like themselves. Hence, Shy Guys tend to congregate with other Shy Guys. As you might imagine, this doesn't exactly lead to a lot of skirt-chasing.

As I have noted, a Shy Guy will look for any excuse to *not* talk to a girl. Talking to a girl could lead to hurt feelings, rejection, and humiliation. Talking to your friends, on the other hand—that's safe. That's easy. You know exactly what you're in for: a night of laughs, talking about old times, and general male bonding. Your friends won't reject you. A Shy Guy will always take the safest path.

When a Shy Guy goes out with his friends, he is surrounded by people he knows and trusts. A Shy Guy does not open himself up to too many new people. The friends he makes tend to be lifelong.

So when a Shy Guy is out with his amigos, he is feeling most protected and secure. Adding an element of the unknown, such as a pretty girl, into this equation upsets the whole balance. It shatters the protective wall the Shy Guy has built up around himself. It has taken something safe and made it unpredictable, and Shy Guys don't like unpredictable. And Shy Guys like routine.

Speaking from personal experience, I can say it is a hell of a lot harder approaching girls when your friends are around. It can be a little intimidating. Instead of gaining support and confidence from his friends, a Shy Guy usually feeds off their fear.

When you approach a girl, you are admitting you are attracted to her. What if your friends don't approve of your choice? Plus, what if you get rejected with all your friends around? How could you ever live that down? Generally, when a Shy Guy goes out with his friends and expresses an interest in a girl, the others pick the girl apart, finding things wrong with her. She's too fat. Her nose is too big. She has ugly feet. Whatever.

All it takes is one negative comment, and the Shy Guy loses interest in the girl forever. If your friend says your girl walks like a duck, that's all you'll be able to think about when you look at her. Once a Shy Guy hears a put-down of his intended girl, he can never look at her the same way again.

This is why I propose going out alone every once in a while. Now, at this point, you're probably asking yourself, "What is he saying? He wants me to abandon my friends?"

Not at all. But if you aren't meeting any women with your friends around, why not try flying solo one night? Do it sometime when your friends aren't around. Go to a bar, a coffee shop, or a party—someplace where you don't know anyone. Sit down by yourself and see what happens.

One of the first things you'll learn about going out alone—especially if you are shy—is that it's intensely, overwhelmingly, mind-numbingly boring. You'll be so bored, you'll be thrilled to talk to the first girl who comes along. Think you can't do it? Think you're still too shy? Never underestimate the power of boredom.

Going out by yourself is so dull, you're bound to meet someone! The need for companionship and conversation will be so intense, you'll find yourself approaching girls you would never dream of talking to if your friends were around.

If you think about it, when hunting for a mate it makes more sense to go out alone. If your friends have the same taste in girls that you do, you'll only wind up competing with them over the same females, and that's not healthy for a friendship. In these situations, nobody wins.

And if your friends go for a different type of girl than you do, they'll probably pick out all the things they don't find attractive about your girl, and convince you not to approach her.

As for the classic situation of two guys approaching two girls and both couples hitting it off—come on, let's be realistic here. The odds of two gals being attracted to two guys and vice versa, are so astronomical, they're almost non-existent. Most likely, at least one of the four people is going to be disappointed. Maybe even two. The best you can hope for in these situations is that your friend supports you by making friendly conversation with the girl he has no real interest in, knowing that you would do the same for him.

Another problem is that no two friends can agree on when it is time to bail. If you think you are hitting it off with a girl and your friend wants to move on, this creates a conflict. Everyone knows what it's like to be someplace where they don't want to be. I know I have a high boredom factor. When I go out, I get bored easily and often want to go someplace else. Likewise, if I'm chatting up a girl and my friends are left on the sidelines, they get restless and want to move on.

Now you're stuck with a dilemma. Do you stay with the girl and try to make a good thing last, or do you try to play Loyal Friend and go with your buddies to another place? This is the type of potential conflict you face every time you go out with your buddies looking for a mate.

If you go out by yourself, you don't have to worry about this problem. If you meet a girl you like, you can stay with her until closing. If you're not having any luck, you can hit the road. You can even go check out those dive bars that your friends can't stand. The only downside to going out by yourself is that girls will wonder why a great catch like you is hanging out alone. The first thing they will ask you is: who are you with?

There are a couple of things you can do in this situation. They all involve lying. The first lie is this: "I'm meeting some friends here." This is a good one, because it provides a logical explanation as to why you are in a bar by yourself. You can even play it off like your friends are a bunch of deadbeats who probably won't show up. Say something like, "They were supposed to be here at 11:00, but it looks like they're not going to make it."

The girl may then take pity on you and decide to keep you company for the rest of the night. I know what you're thinking here: do I really need to resort to artificial pity to get a date? I say, use whatever works for you! As Homer Simpson once said, "Ah, sweet pity! Where would my love life have been without you?"

The second lie is, "My friends are shooting pool in the next room" or "My friends are downstairs watching the band" or "My friends are on the dance floor." In this way, you create the illusion that you came with a big group of people and you just happen to be separated from them at this moment. Make like your friends have a one-track mind. "All those guys ever want to do is shoot pool! But I wanted to listen to the band."

The tricky part here is if the girl asks you to point your friends out to her. The secret to this technique is to pick a large club, with several rooms or floors. You always want to tell her, "My friends are in the other room"—whichever room you're not in. You also want to make sure the girl doesn't see you entering or leaving the club, because then she'll know you lied. If you time it right, you can arrive before her and leave long after she has gone.

The third lie is to make up some big story about where your friends are—"They all went to the big concert tonight and I couldn't get a ticket," or "I had to work late and I couldn't go," or whatever. This creates a valid excuse for you to be out by yourself. Create the illusion that you wish you were out with your friends, but circumstances prevented it.

The most important thing is to let the girl know you have a lot of friends and generally hang out with them, but this is the one time in your life you went out by yourself.

Whatever you do, don't let on that you came out by yourself hoping to pick up girls. This is the last thing any girl wants to hear. It makes you sound like some kind of slick pickup artist who gets his kicks out of cruising for chicks. Girls really do not want to hear that. There are some situations where the truth is the last thing you want to resort to. This is one of them.

You want her to think you are a nice, normal, guy with a lot of friends, who just happens not to have his friends around him at this moment. You do not want her to think you are some kind of solo stalker, who hunts alone in pursuit of prey.

Because if she gets that idea in her head, brother, it's all over!

Personal Ads!

Let's say you've read my advice on how to meet girls, but you still find my methods a little bold for your tastes. You just don't have it in you to approach a strange girl. That's okay. It's not unusual for a Shy Guy. It's entirely possible that you may never reach the point where you can walk up to a total stranger and start up a conversation. Some Shy Guys go their whole lives without ever doing it.

I know how hard it can be. I've been there. It's not a very natural thing to talk to some girl you don't even know; you have to seem interesting and clever and try not to embarrass yourself while, at the same time, evaluating whether you really are interested in her and she really is interested in you . . . It can be a bit intimidating.

If this is the case with you, you may want to consider the personal ads. I have never taken out or answered a personal ad, and I'll tell you why. I place a very high value on physical attraction. When you deal with personal ads, you may spend hours on the phone with a girl, running up huge phone bills, only to find when you meet her in person that she's just not your type. That means all those hours you spent on the phone, picturing your Dream Girl on the other end, were just a big waste of time.

My friend Steve met a French girl through the personals who described herself as "very attractive." After a couple weeks of talking on the phone, Steve and the French girl finally arranged to meet in a bar. I happened to be present when they met, and believe me, this girl was *not* "very attractive." Calling her "very average" would be generous.

When he first arrived at the bar, Steve was standing right next to this girl, but he figured there was no way this Plain Jane could be the "very attractive" French girl he had talked to on the phone. When she finally spoke up and he realized who she was, Steve bailed on her as fast as possible. He didn't want to spend another minute with a girl he had absolutely no attraction to.

The problem with personal ads is that people tend to exaggerate to try to make themselves sound like good catches. So a plain girl becomes "pretty," a pretty girl becomes "beautiful," and even an ugly girl becomes "attractive."

When a young lady is ready to take out a personal ad, she looks through all the other ads in the newspaper, sees every other girl describing herself as gorgeous, and feels her own description must equal or top the others. It just wouldn't do to be the only "cute" girl on a page where all the other girls are "extremely beautiful."

Every girl wants to be the best car on the lot. A girl taking out a personal ad faces a lot of competition, so she may find it necessary to spice up her ad a little bit to catch the reader's eye. She really has to sell herself, using the slickest Madison Avenue jargon she knows.

That's why I don't trust the personal ads. Some girls are not above lying to trick a guy into dating them. Now they may not see it as lying—it is possible that every girl in the world considers herself "very attractive," in her own way. But keep in mind, there is no one policing the personals. A girl can describe herself as "hotter than Cindy Crawford, Claudia Schiffer, and Tyra Banks rolled into one," and there are no personal ad cops to enforce the truth in advertising laws here. Sadly, lying in a personal ad is not a punishable offense. If there were some kind of panel that could verify the truth and accuracy of every ad, and rate the attractiveness of the person placing it, then I would have more faith in this method of meeting girls.

Watch out for any woman who describes herself as "full-figured," "generously proportioned," or "voluptuous." This usually means the girl is overweight. And you especially want to watch out for any girl who doesn't describe her figure at all. On a page full of women who describe themselves as "thin," "slender," and "athletic," a girl who doesn't describe her body is probably pleasantly plump. Not that there's anything wrong with that, but it's important to know what you're getting.

As a general rule, most women who place personal ads tend to be in their late twenties and up. These are women who have soured on singles bars and are tired of being preyed on by pickup artists in smoky nightclubs. Usually, their ads start out, "Tired of the bar scene . . ." Often they are divorced and have children, and want you to know it up front.

Basically, they are gals who have given up hope of meeting anyone face-to-face, and are resorting to the personals as a last resort. They are at the end of their social rope, so to speak. My own feeling is, I'd rather not meet anyone who is desperate and has lost faith in men. I'm still a firm believer in the idea that a guy and a girl can meet face-to-face, strike up a conversation based on a mutual attraction, and build a relationship from there.

Having said all that, I will admit that several of my Shy Guy friends have had great success with personal ads. In fact, two of my best friends are currently in long-term relationships with girls they met through the personals.

My friend Charlie is a long-time believer in personal ads. He's the King of the Classifieds. Over the years, he has placed dozens of his own ads, and answered hundreds more. Charlie tells me that most people who place ads are guys, and that when a girl places an ad, she tends to get dozens of responses. When a fella places an ad, he may get only a small handful of responses, or none at all.

Charlie once told me a story of a girl who got so many responses to her ad, she had the luxury of sifting through all her messages and narrowing down her prospects to the two or three she liked best—and she actually told every guy who called her that she was doing this! It is my understanding that guys usually don't have that option when they place an ad—you're pretty much limited to the two or three responses you get, if that.

Charlie has had more luck with personal ads than most guys. His last three relationships came from the classifieds. One of them lasted four and a half years, most of which he spent living with the girl. The second lasted about ten months, but was cut short when his girlfriend died. The third went so well that he married the girl after dating her for only a year!

Charlie first met his new wife at a poetry reading and they had a mutual attraction, though neither did anything about it at the time. Later, when she answered Charlie's personal ad, neither knew that they had already met. Shortly before they arranged to get together, they began to suspect they had met before. I'll let Charlie take it from here. "We were both rather surprised to see that we already knew each other. It was a great icebreaker. And we had the advantage of knowing we were already attracted to each other." (It's kind of like that "piña colada" song, where the guy responds to a classified ad, thinking he's going to meet a new babe, only to find that the ad was placed by his girlfriend!)

Charlie said that the more of his personality that he showed in his ads, the more success he had. "I used to place generic ads, and not have much luck with them. I was getting generic responses from generic women. Then I started to get picky. I got more specific about who I was, and I became more choosy about the ads I was responding to. The best advice I could have for your readers is to just be honest, be yourself."

If you write a really quirky, offbeat ad, you may not get as many responses as you would from a generic ad, but the ones you do get will be choice. As Charlie put it, "It's better to get five responses from women you have a lot in common with than twenty responses from people you have nothing in common with."

I asked Charlie which is better—responding to other people's ads, or waiting for them to respond to yours.

He answered, "Responding to ads is harder. There's that whole feeling that you're being auditioned by the other person. It's like a job interview."

If you plan on answering some personal ads, Charlie also advises you to be open-minded. That's how he met his wife, a smoker with a daughter. "I never thought I would answer an ad from a smoker. She also has an eight-year-old child. But I decided that these are unimportant things. What's important is how the woman is emotionally. Is she affectionate, spiritual—the deep, inside things."

You may also want to have a good bank account. For one thing, many girls in their twenties are looking for a man whom they describe as "financially secure," though Charlie says "I would never go out with a woman who judges a man by his income," and I agree with that.

For another thing, answering ads can get very expensive. First you listen to the girl's outgoing message, and that costs two dollars a minute. Then you leave a message for her, and that also costs two dollars a minute. You figure you want to talk about yourself for at least a few minutes, to give the girl some idea of what your personality is like. Sometimes the girl's outgoing message can run a few minutes, too. If you leave messages with three or four different girls, that can really start to add up. Charlie tells me there were times when he was spending up to 150 to 200 dollars a month just answering personal ads, and many of his messages were left with girls who never called back.

Usually the personal ad people try to lure you in by allowing you to place your own ad for free. What they don't tell you is that it costs you two dollars a minute to retrieve a message that's been left for you. It even costs you money to call and find out you have no messages! Think how depressing that is—you're spending money to find out that nobody wants you!

As Charlie notes, the desperation factor comes into play here. Usually an equal number of guys and girls take out personal ads. Ads don't cost anything, after all. But when it comes to actually spending money to answer other people's ads, that's where the gents far outnumber the ladies. Guys are far more willing to spend money to meet someone than girls are. Girls just don't get nearly as desperate as guys do. Sometimes I think that men are from one planet—I dunno, let's say, Pluto—and women are from a completely different planet—maybe Uranus—but that's a whole other subject entirely. Besides, I think someone has already written that book.

Basically, a girl can sort through her responses as if she were a customer in a seafood restaurant, looking over the lobsters in a tank, and picking the one she likes best.

There is one distinct advantage for a Shy Guy using the personals, though: It's a helluva lot easier for a Shy Guy to pounce on an ad than it is to pounce on a real live chick. With a personal ad, you know the girl is looking to meet someone, and all you have to do is leave a message on her voice mail. If she likes your message, she will call you. It's much easier than risking rejection face-to-face.

Charlie says that after you've spent some quality phone time with a girl, the next step is to set up a face-to-face meeting with each other, something casual, for drinks or coffee. Choose a neutral meeting spot, halfway between your two homes. Get together and talk to each other for a little while, and, if she turns out not to be what you expected, tell her, "It was nice meeting you, but I have to go." Make up an appointment that you can't miss.

The first meeting is an important one, and will generally determine if you will ever see this girl again. If she bails after one cup of coffee, she is probably not interested. But if she stays for a second cup, and then suggests the two of you get together again sometime, you're in like Flynn.

One good test to use in this situation is to suggest a change of scenery. After you finish your drinks, ask her if she wants to do something else—take a walk, grab a bite to eat, whatever. Her response to this may determine your future with her. If she eagerly agrees to move on to a new location, that's a good sign.

That means she's comfortable being around you and enjoys your company. But if she says, "I have to run. I've got a lot of things to do today," you may want to start scanning the personals again.

For all my bad-mouthing of personal ads, they are, in theory, the ideal way to meet your perfect girl. When looking for a mate, one of the most important things is finding someone who shares your interests. With personal ads, you're able to learn, before you even meet, if you and your girl have anything in common. It eliminates a lot of the guesswork involved when you meet someone the old-fashioned way. When you first approach a girl at a party, for instance, all you have to go on is physical attraction. You have no idea about this girl's life. What are her hobbies? What's her personality like? Is she even single?

A personal ad takes away that element of uncertainty. You know she's single, you know what her interests are, you have a vague idea of what she looks like, and you get to speak to her on the phone before you meet, to determine whether the two of you are are compatible.

In many cases, people who answer personal ads even send each other photos before they meet to see if there is a physical attraction. My problem with this method is that it could take you weeks to find out that you don't even have a physical attraction to a girl; whereas, if you had met her face-to-face, you would have known instantly. Also, photos can lie. Is it a recent photo? Does it show her entire figure? Beware of those photos that only show girls from the waist up. She may have one king-sized caboose!

But if you are willing to take that risk, personal ads are a great way for a Shy Guy to meet a girl. I don't really condone this method, because it won't help you get over your shyness, but it might get you a girlfriend, and that's more important in the long run.

The Internet: The Singles Bar of the Future

I must admit that at first, I was baffled by the idea of people wanting to meet each other over the Internet. You can't even see the face of the person you are talking to. You don't know if she's pretty or ugly, young or old, fat or skinny—or, for that matter, female! According to an article in my favorite newspaper, *USA Today*, experts estimate that "two out of three 'women' in many chat rooms, particularly the sex oriented ones, are men."

Just like with personal ads, it's far too easy to make up stuff about yourself when chatting with someone online.

Since just about everybody who goes online lies about something, odds are the person you're talking to is making up a few things, too. Think about the ridiculousness of this situation. You're lying to her, she's lying to you, and you both think you're meeting somebody really interesting! What kind of way is that for two people to meet each other?

These days, newspapers are full of stories about people who have perpetrated hoaxes over the Internet. First there were stories of "gangsta web sites," which supposedly were recruiting new members online to spread a wave of death and destruction. The gangsta web sites turned out to be a hoax by one guy with a lot of free time on his hands. This nutty prankster managed to fool the wire services and major newspapers of the world.

In another instance, a boy ran away from home to meet with a girl he had met online who lived thousands of miles away. The boy's parents acted fast and called the cops, who nabbed the kid at the airport before he left town. A police investigation revealed that the address the boy was heading to was phony, and the girl did not really exist.

In a third example, a dirty old man posed as a fifteen-year-old boy online, and tricked a fifteen-year-old girl into sending him explicit photos of her. He was arrested and charged with soliciting child pornography.

These are just three examples of online deceptions. I'm sure there are hundreds more. Of course, there are some honest people online, too, but it is easy to fool people in cyberspace. There's no guarantee you're ever going to actually meet the people you are chatting with online, so what's your incentive to tell the truth?

Recently, a friend of mine became obsessed with meeting girls on the Internet, and he put the whole experience in perspective for me for the very first time. When I commented to him that he didn't really know anything about the girls he was talking to, he informed me that was the whole point.

The magic of the Internet is that it's a world of fantasy, where nothing is real. A Shy Guy can be superaggressive. A quiet, mousey girl can be sexy, alluring, and daring. People can say things they would never say in real life. They can talk about wild fantasies and kinky behavior, and reveal things about themselves they wouldn't even tell their best friends.

Total anonymity. That is the secret of the Internet. Nothing is as it seems. That beautiful eighteen-year-old girl you're with in the chat room may actually be a sixty-five-year-old fat guy, but you'll never know it. For a few brief minutes, she is your fantasy come true.

That's why people love the Internet so much. That trashy Jersey girl with the no-class accent can become a sexy Japanese geisha, ready to satisfy all your desires. An overweight girl who wouldn't even get a second look on the street can become a *Playboy* centerfold, with guys lining up to chat with her. A timid secretary can become a dangerous dominatrix, waiting to whip you into submission.

The only limitation is how fast you can type.

The Internet is really the ultimate place for Shy Guys to meet girls. It is a place where you can talk to girls all across the world, without ever having to meet them face-to-face. Think about it. You can be anyone. Do anything. You can tell stories about people you've never met. You can pretend to be fabulously wealthy. You can make up incredible adventures and pretend that they really happened to you.

And most important, you can talk to hundreds of females without ever having to look them in the eye.

To a Shy Guy, there is no better way to pick up girls.

Of course, I frown on the Internet as a way of meeting someone. It's just not the way to go if you ever intend to get over your shyness. Just like with personal ads, I see this as the easy way out. Meeting somebody in person is a little more challenging—and ultimately rewarding—than doing it over the Internet or through personal ads.

Now, at this point, I can hear you saying, "But people can send each other photos over the Internet, so you can see what she really looks like!"

That idea works, in theory. But, as noted earlier, photos can lie. The girl may have put on a hundred pounds since the picture was taken. That photo may not even be her. It may be her friend, or a picture from a magazine. Pictures transmitted over the Internet tend to not be of very high quality. They can be grainy and out of focus. Being a cynic at heart, I wouldn't trust any picture sent over the Internet.

And even if you do like the picture, that still doesn't mean you're going to like the girl. There's so much more to a girl than looks. There's her voice. The way she walks. The way she laughs. The way her perfume smells. How often she bathes. Her mannerisms. Any one of these things can be enough to turn you off completely.

Let me put it this way: if Fran Drescher of TV's *The Nanny* sent her picture over the Internet, most guys would go for her in a heartbeat. When they actually met her in person, they would be so turned off by her grating, whiny voice, they would run from her like Superman from kryptonite. That's why I place such a high value on face-to-face meetings. You need to see the whole package to find out exactly what you're getting. You wouldn't buy a car from an ad in a magazine.

One night I observed as my buddy went online, just to see what type of girls are out there. The first thing I noticed is that there is a preponderance of eighteen-year-old girls on the Internet, just waiting to meet guys. At first, I was suspicious. I couldn't believe there were actually so many eighteen-year-old girls out there desperate to meet men online.

My gut told me many of these eighteen-year-old girls were actually fifty-year-old men. Then I interviewed some real teenage girls in person, not over the net. Much to my surprise, I found that teenage girls really do enjoy going online to talk to men.

It seems there's a very computer-literate generation growing up out there. Many young people have access to computers, either at home, school, or work. Just as teenage girls of years ago enjoyed talking on the phone, young girls these days enjoy going online with strangers. The Internet is the modern equivalent of the C.B. radio we used to have in the seventies.

The big difference is that the girls who go online seem to not take it very seriously, whereas the guys trying to pick them up are very serious. Girls do it as a kick, something to kill time. It's safe flirting for our generation.

One teenage girl I spoke to said she likes helping guys get their rocks off by engaging in cybersex with them online, though she swears she does not pleasure herself during these sessions. Today's high school girls would probably never talk to a strange older man in public, but behind the safety of a computer monitor, it becomes a harmless after-school activity.

One night, my friend Steve went online and asked, as he always does, if there were any single women out there looking to meet anyone. A girl named "Becky" logged on, saying she would love to chat. At first, Steve was thrilled. Steve was a car buff, and Becky knew a lot about cars.

As they chatted some more, Becky revealed she was a cop.

She also revealed she was a guy.

Steve logged off real quick!

On another night, Steve was chatting online with a girl who said she lived nearby, was beautiful, blonde, and desperate for sex. She begged Steve to come over right then, that night, and satisfy her.

Fortunately, Steve had enough common sense not to go. It's a pretty safe bet it would not have been a woman who was sexy, desperate, and horny. No beautiful girl ever has to beg for sex, and even if she did, she certainly wouldn't do it over the Internet.

Odds are it was some fat, sweaty guy sitting around the house in his underwear. Sorry to burst your bubble there, netheads, but this is the real world, and it's not nearly as pretty as cyberspace! My friend Steve insists that by asking the right questions, a savvy net-surfer can screen out the phonies and locate the actual girls. The cynic in me says that anyone can give the right answers if they watch enough MTV.

So until the day when every person on the Internet is able to see and hear everyone else, I'll avoid the Internet. (From what I understand about new technology, this day is coming soon!) But if you're a Shy Guy who is just beginning to come out of his shell, the Internet is a great way to start you off on your road to becoming a sociable guy.

This type of role-playing can be harmless fun—call it mental masturbation, if you will—but it can also be dangerous if you get carried away and the Internet becomes your entire social life. There's nothing wrong with chatting with girls online, but make sure to set up actual meetings with some of these girls, so you can make sure your online girlfriend is what she says she is. See if she wants to take your relationship out of cyberspace into the real world. There are a couple of web sites that are particularly popular for matchmaking. One is called Love @ AOL (America Online), which allows you to view the photo personal ads of more than 30,000 people. Another sight, Match.com showcases 85,000 members. Both of these sites seem ideal for meeting computer-literate singles.

And if you want to engage in cybersex, that's okay, too. Personally, I can't endorse any kind of sex that involves holding your Johnson in one hand and a mouse in the other.

Singles Dances

The singles dance. It sounds like a Shy Guy's idea of heaven. An entire dancehall filled with single girls, each of them looking to hook up. Think about it. No one goes to a singles dance unless they are looking to meet someone. When you go to a regular bar, probably 98 percent of the girls there have no intention of meeting anyone. Ah, but a singles dance—it's as if every girl there has a sign on her that says, "Available!" This is a perfect situation for a Shy Guy, because the risk factor is reduced to almost nothing.

With that thought in mind, I decided to attend my first singles dance. It was something I had avoided, because these events reek of desperation, just like personal ads and dating services. Going to a singles dance is like admitting to the world, "OK, I give up. I admit I'm no good at meeting girls. I can't do this the normal way. Bring in a barrelful of fish and I'll start shooting."

But after you've been single long enough, you do start to get a little desperate and willing to try new approaches. I finally reached a point where my curiosity got the better of me, so a buddy and I went to our first singles dance.

We lasted about five minutes. We didn't even get in the door before realizing we were the only people there under the age of fifty. We knew we were in trouble when the guy at the door said they were offering a senior citizen's discount. I haven't seen that much gray hair since I stopped watching *Matlock*! Those folks at the singles dance were amazing. They danced all night, and never got up from their wheelchairs! Every guy wants to meet a girl who's just like his mom. These girls were more like your grandmother! They knew all the latest dances—the Charleston, the Lindy . . . They would have danced all night, but the curfew at their rest home was ten o'clock!

My experience with singles dances was a disaster. I walked away and never looked back. My old pal, Charlie, has had a much more positive experience with singles dances than I have. (Yes, this is the same guy from the earlier section on Personal Ads. Charlie is my resident authority on Unconventional Methods of dating.) Charlie prefers his females to be in the thirty-five-plus age range, which is exactly the age group you find at these things.

Charlie has met several women at singles dances. But it isn't always easy for him to close a deal at these little soirees, because many of the women see him as too young. He's in his early thirties.

I asked Charlie if singles dances were worthwhile for a Shy Guy.

Right off the bat, Charlie noted a couple of important things about singles dances. "First of all, they get you out of the house. Second, they get you one step closer to your goal of meeting someone. The people there are usually friendly. I'd say one out of two times, I'd come home with a phone number. But it helps to like women over forty, like I do.

"Even though some singles dances specifically attempt to attract people in their twenties and thirties, young people still go to bars and clubs. Most people at singles dances are in their forties or late fifties.

"Unfortunately, even if you do like older women, many are still surprisingly resistant to the idea of dating younger men."

Charlie told me one of the things he likes best about singles dances: "Just about anybody can ask anybody to dance. Usually in a bar, a lot of women are resistant to the idea of dancing with strangers, because it is expected to lead to phone numbers and dates. But at a singles dance, women will gladly give you one dance, and then you never see them again.

"Another good thing is that there are a surprising number of women who enjoy slow dancing."

Charlie told me he once attended a singles dance that was advertised as being for people aged twenty-five to forty-nine, "but still, most people were in their late thirties." Another time, a dance was divided into two rooms, one for young people, one for older people. "But so many more old people showed up than younger people that the younger people felt uncomfortable hanging out in a mostly empty room, so everyone wound up going into the old people's room."

Charlie analyzed the difference between personal ads and singles dances. "Singles dances are less expensive than answering personal ads. There is the advantage of being able to see what the people look like. Personal ads concentrate more on common values and interests, rather than on looks.

"One of the disadvantages of singles dances is that personal ads allow me to look for someone deep, unusual, uncommon. Singles dances tend to attract a more conventional crowd. Another advantage of personal ads is that they tend to attract a younger crowd. You tend to find people in their earlier thirties."

As far as the types of music you'll hear at a singles dance, Charlie says, "They play all types of music, from seventies disco to current club songs. A singles dance is a good place to go if you like the Macarena. It's almost like a cross between a disco and a wedding. One minute you'll be doing the electric slide, the next minute you'll be doing some seventies disco dance."

Charlie feels that a singles dance offers a good opportunity for a Shy Guy to meet someone, because "women tend to be friendlier and more open, at least when it comes to talking to people. They don't have their defenses up, like they would in a club. You're never invading anyone's space. It offers you a chance to constantly interact with other people. As something of a Shy Guy myself, I found it provided a good ego boost. I found myself saying some very bold things that I wouldn't normally say."

However, there is always the age difference to consider. One time, a woman told Charlie, "I wish you were ten years older!" On another occasion, a woman informed him, "I'm old enough to be your mother!" Charle then informed the woman that while it was true that she was biologically old enough to be his mother, she would have to have given birth to him when she was fifteen.

Before he settled into a long-term relationship, Charlie developed a philosophy. He would date women who could technically be his mother, but who would have had to become mothers at shockingly young ages. In other words, a woman fifteen years older than him was fine. A woman eighteen years older than him was out of the question. The oldest women he ever went out with was forty-seven to his thirty-one, but it took a lot of convincing on his part to get that date.

Charlie pointed out that it helps to live in an urban area, since that is where most singles events take place. "I live about fifty minutes outside of New York City, and the nearest singles dance is usually about forty-five minutes away. On the other hand, with personal ads, half the time, the person you meet lives about forty-five minutes away, so it's six of one, half a dozen of the other."

Whether you choose either of his two preferred methods—singles dances or personal ads—Charlie recommends that you "try every single way you feel comfortable with. One of them is bound to work. Treat it like a job search. Be methodical. Be determined. Don't sit around waiting for something to happen. Go through the newspaper every week. Tell yourself, 'I'm going to answer four personal ads every week. I'm going to go to one singles dance every week.' My goal has always been to minimize my time out in the single world, and because of this, I haven't been without a relationship for more than a year."

Charlie concluded his thoughts on singles dances by observing, "I haven't been to any of these Jewish singles dances, but there seem to be a lot more of them. Jewish people have a tendency to like to marry within their own religion, so they have a lot more social gatherings like this."

In addition to Jewish singles dances, there are other singles dances that cater to Catholics and various other religions. You just need to find out beforehand exactly which group each particular dance is intended for.

If you are interested in pursuing this method of meeting girls, keep your eyes open for ads in your local paper. Usually every Friday in the lifestyle section, you will see numerous ads for that weekend's singles activities. Some ads actually specify that the event is intended for those thirty or over. Every now and then, you will see an ad promoting a dance that is aimed at those in their twenties.

In addition to dances, there are other singles events you may wish to consider, such as singles movie screenings, nature walks, and cruises. Some cities have monthly magazines that come out especially for singles, listing events and activities, and including personal ads.

Any time you're gathered together with a bunch of people who are all single and desperate, you've got to figure your odds are pretty good. Though I would wager the majority of people attending these things tend to be guys. My ultimate nightmare is to be trapped out at sea on a singles cruise with a couple hundred other single guys and no girls anywhere.

In general, there seem to be singles events held for just about every age, nationality, or religion. There are some some exceptions, though. As far as I know, there are no atheist singles groups. And you satanists are on your own, too!

Dating Services

Okay, finally we come to a subject I know nothing about! Most of the information in this book comes from my own experiences, or those of my friends. Dating Services are uncharted territory for me.

My research told me that there are basically two different types of dating services. The first type is the one people are most familiar with, the video dating service. The one I called has offices in Miami and Boca Raton, Florida.

Their ad in the Yellow Pages brags that their approach works so well, "it resulted in more than two weddings a day last year." That's a pretty impressive statistic. I wonder if they can back it up.

I spoke with an incredibly enthusiastic British woman named Elizabeth. She told me that her service has been around for over twenty-one years, and had over 4,300 single members.

"The first thing I want to make clear," Elizabeth told me, "is that we don't matchmake here. We provide a nice, safe, comfortable environment for quality people to find each other."

I was a little confused to hear this. After all, aren't a dating service and a matchmaking service the exact same thing? If I were looking for a match and the dating service told me, "We're not matchmakers here," I'd probably say, "Oh, I guess you can't help me," and hang up.

Based on Elizabeth's claim to provide a "nice, safe environment" for people to get together, I started to wonder exactly what went on at this place. Maybe this place really was a front for a prostitution ring, like that dating service I saw on *Charlie's Angels*! Further questioning revealed that it was, in fact, a legitmate dating service, and that there was none of that "on-premises dating" going on.

Elizabeth told me, "Beautiful girls walk in here all the time and tell me, 'I don't like sitting in bars any more. I'm not having any luck in the work environment. I'm ready to try something different.' So this is really the only way to go!" (Yeah, right!)

"We have a large variety of programs, catering to people of all ages, from younger people to retirees. We have a professional photography studio, and when you come in, we take four eight-by-ten pictures of you. They come out beautiful, truly beautiful. Usually we have you bring a change of clothes and we take two casual and two formal pictures. Attached to the back of the picture is a full synopsis of your history and background—your likes and dislikes, hobbies, what you're looking for in a partner—so that the person looking at your photo can learn everything about you." (You can learn everything about me from a one-page outline? Yikes! I guess I'm not as deep as I thought I was.)

"If someone likes what they see, then they take down your video and watch it. And then you watch their video, as well. This is the most special part of all. You actually get to watch the girl you picked, and hear her voice as she talks to you! And she does the same with your video. This way, when you finally meet each other in person, it's like you already know each other!

"You already know how the other laughs and speaks! It's nothing like a blind date. It's wonderful!"

The way Elizabeth described it, dating services sounded so "special" and "wonderful," it's a wonder more people don't use them. But wait. There's more! Elizabeth guaranteed me that I would get to meet "five women every ten days." The way it works is that females come in, look at your photo and video, and put their name down to meet you. Guys are not given the right of first choice. It is the ladies who are given that privilege here.

You watch their videos, and if you like what you see, then the two of you arrange a meeting. Elizabeth noted that you may choose to decline some of these girls, just based on their photos and resumes. As she put it, "You take down the videos of the ones you really like!" If you check in every ten days or so, Elizabeth promised five more girls will be willing to meet you. And so on.

That's roughly one woman every two days, or 180 women a year! Wow! You'll have so many women, you won't know what to do with them all! This reminds me of that old TV show *Love Connection*, on which all the contestants would say, "I date an average of three times a week." I always thought they were lying to make themselves look good on TV. Who the hell gets three dates a week? Most of the time, you're lucky if you can get one!

Elizabeth did admit that her dating service has more male clients than female. She noted that, for some reason, men tend to go for this sort of thing more than women do. The numbers she gave me were 3,421 men and just over 3,000 women. (This contradicts her initial statement of "4,300 single members," but perhaps she got her numbers screwed up.)

Three thousand beautiful, professional, single females. I like those odds.

The only thing Elizabeth wouldn't tell me was the cost of this "wonderful, incredible" service. She noted that there are so many different programs available to their clients, that I really should come in and meet her before discussing price. Just as I suspected. None of these services provide information on prices over the phone, so you have to figure it's pretty expensive.

My pal Charlie tells me that these services usually want a couple thousand dollars up front for a one-year membership. That's about the same amount Charlie was paying to answer personal ads every month, but, as he points out, with personal ads, you don't have to pay all the money up front. And if you do sign up with a dating service and decide you are not satisfied with it, it can be very difficult to get your money back.

Elizabeth stressed that her service was very selective about who is allowed to join. "We have very upscale, professional members. We screen everyone." In order to become a member, you must have an established bank account and a good relationship with a credit card company. It also helps to be attractive.

This got me thinking: What if you are an unattractive slob with a crappy job but a lot of cash? Are they going to turn you down, because you don't meet their definition of "upscale" and "professional"? For that matter, what if you've got a healthy bank account and an incredible job, but are ugly as sin? Are they going to tell you your money is no good there? I wonder.

The second kind of dating service I looked into is the kind that doesn't use videos. The place I called was also based in Miami. I spoke to a girl named Kelly who stressed, "We are not a dating service. There are no videos and no parties." Ironically, this one was listed in the Yellow Pages under "Dating Services."

Kelly described her service as "personalized contemporary matchmaking." Well, at least they admitted to being matchmakers! She said, "We talk to you in-depth, become familiar with your background, find out what kind of women you would like to meet; then we go on our gut in matching you with people who are appropriate for you.

"We don't want to waste your time. We carefully consider every match. After you go on each date, we receive your feedback, which is crucial to us in helping you find someone. If you sign up for a one-year membership, usually we will find you a match between the first and fifth date."

These people are pretty serious about their matchmaking! The other service didn't give a guarantee like that.

The way this place works is they meet with you for about an hour and a half. They take pictures of you "for their files," though any girls who want to date you will not see your pictures, nor will you see theirs. This is the part I'm skeptical about. What's the point of the pictures if nobody is going to see them? And why would you use a dating service that doesn't even let you see a photo of the girl you're going to date?

Kelly informed me, "Our clients are attractive, professional people. We are extremely selective. You will never, ever be disappointed." (Wow! That's a hard promise to keep! I'm pretty easily disappointed!)

Kelly claimed her dating service is "extremely picky," and will often look outside their own membership to find their clients potential mates. For example, if a woman is looking for a male book-reader, representatives from the service will go down to the Miami Book Fair with "Wanted" posters, and hand them out to eligible bachelors.

These types of searches are apparently pretty common for this particular dating service. "We do all kinds of searches. We went to a boat show to find a man for a widow whose husband had owned a yacht. We received calls up and down the East Coast. We do horse shows . . ."

I asked Kelly about the male/female ratio of her clientele. I was told, "It's about half and half. It varies with the age bracket. As people get older, there are less women available."

Kelly had an interesting philosophy on why more men than women use dating services. She noted, "Men are more practical than women. A man will go to an investment broker to manage his money. He'll go to a real estate broker to find him a home. And he'll come to us to find him a wife. Men just have a real easy time with it."

When you put it that way, it actually sounds quite logical. Why should you waste your time in bars or supermarkets, chasing girls you may have absolutely nothing in common with, when you can hire a service to match you up with someone who is your perfect mate in every way?

The only problem is that it seems so mechanical. It's like being matched up by a computer. Kind of takes some of the spontaneity out of things, if you know what I mean. It loses that whole discovery process, that feeling of being pleasantly surprised to find an attractive girl with whom you share some common interests.

On the other hand, it could save you a lot of wasted time.

The only thing Kelly wouldn't tell me over the phone was the cost for this service. She informed me, "That's not my department. You'd have to come down here and meet with our people and they would discuss that with you." I'll say one thing for these dating services: They sure try hard to get you to go down there. I'm sure the thinking is, once they have you inside their doors, you'll feel obligated to sign up.

If you are interested in pursuing the Dating Service option, it would seem the best thing to do is to shop around, and see who has the best prices, the biggest selection of women, and the best methods. If you are a shallow guy like me, you'd want to go for the video dating service. If you are far more trusting than I am, then you could go for the other kind of service—the kind that doesn't offer you a look at your dates beforehand.

But if you're not embarrassed by the idea of telling people, "My wife and I met through a dating service" and you've got extra cash burning a hole in your pocket, go for it. It seems ideally suited to the Shy Guy mentality.

Oh yeah. There is one other type of dating service I should mention. I saw an ad in the Yellow Pages for a service that offered the intriguing concept of "temporary, short-term dating," but this turned out to be a front for a prostitution service, just like that one I saw on *Charlie's Angels*. I was given a price of $190 an hour for a dancer or an escort who will come right to your home. Of all the services I called, this was the only one willing to quote me a price!

But they wouldn't let me see any photos, either!

Chapter Nine

Desperate Methods

In this chapter, we're going to get into methods of meeting girls that are completely shameless. Sure, some of the other methods discussed previously may have had an air of desperation to them, but in this chapter we're going to throw dignity to the wind and let desperation rule the day.

We're going to assume here for a minute that you've tried all my previous methods, and they're not working for you. Never fear. The methods discussed in this chapter will allow you to work around your shyness completely.

Dogs and Babies

Fact: Most girls love dogs and babies. Even the most beautiful, the most unapproachable girls in the world have been known to stop dead in their tracks at the sight of a cute pooch or a precocious toddler. No female can resist the power of a dog or a baby. There is an uncontrollable force in the universe that compels chicks to fuss over anything cuddly.

It doesn't matter how unattainable the girl is. She simply can't help herself. She cannot let a dog or baby pass by without making some effort to touch it, to play with it, to establish some sort of maternal bond.

At this point, you may be wondering, "How does this relate to me, the Shy Guy?" Well, I was just getting to that. Patience, son.

Dogs and babies are the Shy Guy's two best friends. They are your secret weapons in the battle of the sexes.

All you need to do is take a walk through the park with a dog or a baby, and any girl in the world can be yours. You'll just be strolling along, minding your own business, when suddenly the girl of your dreams will come over and start fawning over your dog or baby.

Then it's up to you to make your move. The dog or baby can only take you so far. Once the girl takes your bait, it's up to you to reel her in. She'll probably have lots of questions. This is great, because for once, it puts the girl in the role of Clueless Girl, and you get to be the Answer Man. The most important thing here is that you come across as somebody who really loves children and animals.

Now, the question arises, where do you get these dogs and babies from? If you don't own a dog, maybe you have a friend or neighbor who will let you walk theirs. Maybe you can get a part-time job working for one of those dog-walking services for snooty rich people.

As for babies, well, this is the one time in your life when it pays to be a divorced dad. If you have recently been divorced and you have a couple of kids, you can use those kids to your advantage! When you pick them up on Saturday afternoon, take them to the park, where your prospects are best for prowling. Those kids that you once considered liabilities can actually become assets. Don't think of them as the costly, unwanted products of a union that went sour. Think of them as the bait that helps you land a good catch!

But what if your relationship crumbled before you squeaked out a couple of rug rats? Should you then proceed to kidnap someone else's baby, borrow it for a few hours, and then return it? Well, as logical a solution as that may seem, I really must discourage it, since kidnapping is a felony.

This creates a problem. Where do you get the baby? After all, it's not like you can just go to a store and buy one, like a dog. Well, okay, I guess technically, you could adopt one, or buy one on the black market, but let's not do anything *really* desperate here. You have enough trouble meeting girls. Let's not worry about raising a kid until we've figured out how to talk to girls first, okay?

The best thing you can do here is borrow some nieces or nephews for a little while. Whenever he would walk to the local convenience store, my brother always made sure he took my five-year-old stepsister along with him. He met lots of girls this way.

The important thing is that you bring something young and cute with you out to a public place. No matter how shy you are, a dog or a baby can serve as a magnet to attract babes like nobody's business! If you could get a dog and a baby at the same time, well, there's no telling what could happen! And if you bring a puppy, which is like a dog and a baby all rolled into one . . . well, let's just say you're going to need a pretty big stick to beat all the girls off with!

But borrowing a friend's dog, walking your sister's baby, doesn't all this seem a little, shall we say, deceitful? Well, yes, a little bit. But not too much. It's not like you're renting a fancy car, or borrowing some rich guy's apartment, and acting like you're some carefree millionaire to impress girls. All you're doing is going out in public with something that is bound to attract females. If you're going fishing, you've got to bring some worms, right?

Some of you may feel a little uncomfortable with all this deception, for most Shy Guys are basically decent and honest at heart. Some of you may be saying, "Is it really necessary for me to resort to all this trickery just to meet a girl?"

I can answer that question in one word: Yes! It is necessary! Obviously you need something to improve your chances, otherwise you wouldn't even be reading this chapter!

There's a lot of competition out there in the dating world. You're going up against guys who are bigger than you, wealthier than you, better-looking than you, funnier than you. You need every advantage you can get. Anything you can use to lure a prospective date is fair. Anything that gives you a leg up on the competition; anything you can do to say, "Hey, nice lady! Don't pay any attention to those other losers! Ignore them! Look at me! I'm the only man for you! I have so much more to offer!"

If only there were a service that rents out dogs and babies for leisurely strolls through the park, we Shy Guys would be sitting on top of the world!

The Piggyback Method

Here we come to my least favorite method for meeting girls—the Piggyback Method. This is the way it works: If you are a Shy Guy, find some guy who is not shy and latch on to him socially, taking full advantage of his aggressiveness with girls.

For instance, if you know a guy who gets invited to a lot of parties, start tagging along. It doesn't matter whether you are invited or not. Just go. This may seem a rather bold move to you—attending parties you haven't been invited to—but making bold moves is the beginning of your journey from wimp to manhood!

If you have a friend who is a real superstud, tag along with him whenever he goes out, and try to mooch off whatever girls he approaches. Sometimes your friend may approach two girls at once, and he may throw you the one he likes least. You may laugh now, but a lot of history's greatest romances got started because some guy had a hot chick's average-looking friend handed to him.

If you have a friend who is extremely aggressive about picking up girls, why not ask him to pick one up for you? Here's one possible way to do it. Have your friend approach a girl and say, "See my friend over there? Maybe you can help him out. It's his birthday, and he's a little down because he just broke up with his girlfriend. All he wants is somebody to talk to." It's hard for a girl to resist a good sob story like that. It's okay to tell a few white lies if it helps you overcome your shyness.

Most Hollywood actors are actually very shy. The reason they become actors is because they get to play different parts, assume different personas, that are completely the opposite of their own. Sometimes it helps to pretend you are an actor, playing a part, when you are trying to meet girls. The girl is your audience, and when you stand before her, you are on stage. Depending on your performance, you will either get a standing ovation, or you will get gonged.

Now, let me tell you why I am not fond of the Piggyback Approach. Basically, I am a former Shy Guy who overcame his shyness all by himself (with a little help from TV). I never had anybody else I could mooch girls off of.

Once I overcame my shyness, all my Shy Guy friends wanted to glom onto me whenever I was in a situation where I could meet girls. So instead of me talking to a girl one on one, suddenly I'm talking to a girl with all of my friends standing around me, trying to join in on the conversation. (Since the hardest thing for any Shy Guy is to break the ice, if somebody else breaks the ice first, that gives every other Shy Guy in the vicinity an opportunity to jump into the water!) As you might imagine, it can be difficult to work under these conditions. It's hard enough to meet a girl under ordinary circumstances. It's even harder when you have to compete with your friends for the girl's attention.

There are enough girls in the world. You shouldn't have to fight with your friends for them. You face enough competition from all the Aggressive Guys out there. A Shy Guy needs his friends to support him, not compete with him.

I think it's important to be a supportive friend. It's much harder for a Shy Guy to hook up than it is for an Aggressive Guy, so Shy Guys need every advantage they can get. If you are trying to meet a girl, your friends should not interfere, and you should be respectful of their attempts to hook up. If your friend needs a little time alone with a girl to bust a hard rap, give him his space. Take a walk. Find some way to amuse yourself.

The last thing your friend needs is you butting into the conversation. You'll only distract him, make him feel uncomfortable, and cause him to blow it. It's important for Shy Guys to work together, and not trip all over each other. If your friend sees a girl first, let him have first crack at her. If he strikes out, then you can move in on her. But give your friend room to work. It's only fair. You would expect the same courtesy from him. If you feel the need to join in the conversation, at least have the decency to step aside at the end of the night to allow your friend a chance to get the seven digits.

I liken the situation to prospecting for gold. If you find a gold mine, your friends can help you mine it, but they must understand that the gold is yours. In other words, the person who finds the girl should, by all rights, be the person who gets the girl—unless the girl specifically chooses otherwise.

So that's why I'm not crazy about the Piggyback Method. I'm a big believer in doing things yourself. If your friend is doing all the work, and you're just along for the ride, then you're not really working very hard to overcome your shyness. And you're not really learning how to do it on your own. When your friend is not around, you'll find yourself floundering like a fish out of water.

It's good for beginners. It can get you in the habit of talking to girls and meeting new people, but, ultimately, you can only ride on someone else's coattails for so long before you have to chart your own course.

As long as we're talking about methods I'm not crazy about, I may as well mention what I call the Conversation Crutch. On any given night, there is usually one expression you can use which becomes the "catch phrase" of the night. This is the one word or phrase that is guaranteed to get a laugh from your social circle every time you say it.

Like my old pal Warren Mateychak says, when someone has no real personality or sense of humor, they will simply find one line they think is funny and repeat it all night. As a writer, I hate to rely on the Conversation Crutch, because it is just too damned easy.

Here's an example, overheard in a bar. A couple of guys were putting the moves on some girls they had never met. Nearby, there was a hot dog vendor, whose cart was emblazened with the name "Lucky Dog." That became the catch phrase of the night for those two guys.

Whenever conversation began to lag, one of the guys would go for the cheap laugh by making a joke about "Lucky Dog." It was pretty much guaranteed that every few minutes, you'd hear one of the guys make a "Lucky Dog" reference. The girls thought it was hysterical. The whole idea here is that the more times you say something, the funnier it is.

I expect better than this from you. If you are a Shy Guy, you are probably clever and original. You are capable of much more than this. However, there is one thing to be said about the Conversation Crutch: it does make it a lot easier to get to know a girl. It gives you a Shared Experience. If she thinks the line is funny, she will be comfortable around you, and she may join you in the joke-making process.

If she thinks you're funny when you use the same tired old catch phrase, wait until she really gets to know you and finds out how clever you really are! So the Conversation Crutch can be an effective way of loosening somebody up, keeping the laughs coming and the conversation flowing. It's cheap, it's easy, and I know you're capable of so much more, but if you feel you must use it . . .

I like to say that you don't need a crutch to walk, but it does make walking a little easier. Eventually, you'll be able to throw the crutch away and walk proudly on your own. But until that day comes . . . well, we've always got Lucky Dog!

Chapter Ten

Blind Dates and Third Wheels

It's inevitable. At some point in your life, you are going to be asked to play the Third Wheel. There is no way to avoid it. It's as inevitable as death, taxes, and Al Bundy sticking his hand down his pants.

There's really no way you can avoid the Third Wheel Syndrome. You'll be sitting around, minding your own business, when some well-meaning couple asks you to join them for some social outing or another. Maybe it's dinner. Maybe it's a movie. Maybe it's (ugh!) both. That feels uncomfortably like a date, where you are Johnny Tag-Along.

Whether or not you choose to go depends on your tolerance for this sort of thing. In my younger days, I reluctantly played Third Wheel a few times, and usually wound up regretting it. Most couples I know are pretty cool about avoiding PDAs (Public Displays of Affection), but, inevitably, there will come a time when they start making goo-goo eyes at each other, and there is nothing for you to do but sit there uncomfortably and be reminded that you have no one.

Another problem I have with hanging out with couples is this: No matter how much the couple may like you and enjoy your company, there is going to come that moment when you start to say something, and they cut you off in mid-sentence and talk to each other. Suddenly you realize just how unimportant you are to this little get-together. One minute, the three of you are equals, the Three Musketeers. One for all, and all for one. The next minute, they're Romeo and Juliet, and you're this tiny, little annoying bug that they step on. It really does a lot for your self-esteem, let me assure you.

When two people are in a couple, there is nothing you or anyone else can say that is more important than what they have to say to each other. My old pal, Warren Mateychak, has a great theory about relationships, which goes like this: When a man and a woman enter into a relationship together, they are essentially forming a partnership in which it's them vs. everyone else in the world.

Whether they intend to or not, couples tend to develop a sort of superiority complex, where they feel better than everyone else, especially the single people. Many couples like to spend their time whispering to each other and making little judgments about the people around them, secure in the knowledge that their union makes them stronger than everyone else.

The one thing couples hate most is to see someone who is alone. They will do anything to get you into a relationship of your own, so they can see you as an equal. Otherwise, you are just an inferior.

Our society cannot accept the idea of a single guy. Everything in life is set up for couples: going to weddings, eating out, riding on a roller coaster. If you've ever sat at a table in a restaurant where every guy at the table had a girlfriend except you, you know firsthand just how lonely the life of a single guy can be.

I try to avoid hanging out with couples whenever possible. I like to be treated as an equal, and when you're with a couple, that's not always possible. I prefer to hang out with other single people, where at least we are all on the same social level, more or less. You don't have to face that awkward moment when a couple starts making out with each other, and you're left standing there, staring off into space, pretending not to notice.

But you don't have to follow my example. It's quite possible you've played Third Wheel in the past and had some very positive experiences. I say if you are comfortable playing Third Wheel, or Fifth Wheel, or Seventh Wheel, or any other odd-numbered wheel, by all means, do so. As you get older, and more and more of your friends enter into couples, you may not have much of a choice!

Now, for all my Third Wheel bashing, there is one good thing to be said about the subject: girls hate playing Third Wheel just as much as guys do, but they seem to be far more willing to do it than guys are.

So the next time you go to a party or a bar, look for the girl who is hanging with the couple. She's probably bored. She's probably being ignored. She probably wishes she were somewhere else.

This is where you come in. Think back on all those times you were stuck playing the Third Wheel and how much you hated it. Then walk over to that girl and save her from a night of misery.

Third Wheel girls are among the very best girls for a Shy Guy to approach. For one thing, you can relate to them—you've been there before. For another thing, they're probably glad to talk to someone other than the couple they came with—anyone! You can help this girl create the illusion that she's with someone, and that will make her feel better.

When you hook up with a Third Wheel girl, perhaps the two of you can even form your own partnership against the world. Now it's your turn to whisper sarcastic comments into each other's ears, and generally feel superior to all those around you.

That's the great thing about being in a couple. When you are united with a girl you like, you are truly invincible. Maybe you can even adopt one of your Shy Guy friends to serve as your own Third Wheel. For as long as there are couples, there must be Third Wheels. It's a scientific fact.

Blind Dates

The Blind Date may seem like a relic from a TV sitcom, but it still happens, even in these enlightened times. It is another one of the inevitable facts of Shy Guy life, along with the Third Wheel Syndrome.

The reason for this is, yet again, all those Happy Loving Couples (as singer Joe Jackson calls them) who can't stand to see a Shy Guy going through life without a partner.

They mean well, these Happy Loving Couples (HLCs) and will do whatever it takes to ensure that the Shy Guy enters into a HLC of his own. All the couples in the world are like a great big Borg collective from *Star Trek: The Next Generation*. When they see a single lifeform, they want to absorb it into their couples culture.

That's what it's like to be a single guy in a world of couples. Couples feel happy and fulfilled, and they want the same thing for you. And they're willing to do whatever it takes to accomplish that goal. Having established my disdain of nonconventional dating methods in the last chapter, you may think I'm the type of person who would never go on a blind date. Not so.

I'll admit that when I first entered the dating pool, I was very much against blind dating, because I took it as a slap in the face from whoever was trying to fix me up. It felt as if the person were saying to me, "You're obviously incapable of doing this on your own, so let me help you."

Once, when I was in my early twenties, my brother tried to set me up on a blind date with a girl he went to college with. He asked me if I'd be interested in going out with her. Even though I was going through a dry spell at the time—I wasn't meeting any girls anywhere, and I hadn't dated in months—I said no. I wasn't interested. It seemed too much like a mercy date. Being young and full of pride, I didn't need anyone's help, or so I thought. My brother let the subject drop. I had made my position very clear.

Later, I got to thinking about that girl. I started to wonder what she looked like, what her likes and dislikes were, what kind of personality she had.

I realized I would never know, because I had passed on my one chance to meet her. I came to regret my hasty decision. I realized I may have turned down an opportunity to meet my perfect girl. For all I know, this girl may have been my soulmate, and I refused to meet her, just because my stubborn sense of pride wouldn't let me accept a blind date.

Gradually, I came to realize that it doesn't matter how you meet someone. You could meet them in the classroom, at work, in a bar, jogging through the park, through mutual friends, through some sort of dating service, or whatever. All that matters is that you meet them. And if you meet someone in a particularly offbeat or interesting way, it can make for an amusing anecdote to tell at parties.

A few years after my initial rejection of the blind date concept, my brother offered me another chance to go on a blind date with a different girl. This time, I accepted without hesitation. My brother knows how picky I am, and I knew he wouldn't set me up with an unattractive girl. If you ever choose to go on a blind date, it is important to establish that the person who arranged the date knows exactly what type of girl you're looking for.

I went on the Blind Date. Actually it was a double date, along with my brother and his girlfriend. My girl turned out to be a cute blonde, definitely my type. I couldn't believe such a pretty girl didn't have a boyfriend. I had definitely lucked out.

If you ever have the chance to go on a Blind Date, you may want to make it a double date, as well. In my case, it helped ease the tension a little, because my girl was with a friend whom she felt comfortable around, and I was with a member of my own family, which enabled me to show a little more personality and act a little more natural. The night went fairly well. I believe it ended with a peck on the lips from my date. After it was over, I told my blind date I would call her, and she said that would be fine. I went home that night satisfied that I had met a pretty, nice girl, who I was definitely interested in seeing again.

I called her a few days later, and left a message. She didn't return my call. I called one more time and left one more message, and that was the end of it. She apparently had no interest in seeing me again. I was disappointed, but I decided it wasn't worth pursuing any further.

Later on, I found out that the girl was going through a very bad breakup with her ex at the time I met her, and was also about to get an abortion. Once I found that out, it was pretty easy to understand why she never called me back. She was going through a very difficult period in her life, and just wasn't looking to start a new relationship at that time. She finally did wind up calling me about a year later. She was alone and needed a date for Valentine's Day.

You might think an experience like that would have soured me on blind dates. Not really. I'm still glad I met her, and at least I got to have one date with her. Even though things didn't work out for us, I had a good time, and any time you go out with a pretty girl, it can only boost your confidence for the next time such an opportunity arises.

So do I recommend blind dates for Shy Guys? Yes, I do. It beats sitting around the house, watching TV. And you never know. The next girl you meet could be your future wife. So the next time you have an opportunity to go on a blind date, why not go for it? Who knows? You might be pleasantly surprised.

Chapter Eleven

A New Image

I check my look in the mirror
I wanna change my clothes, my hair, my face

—BRUCE SPRINGSTEEN, "Dancing in the Dark"

Have you ever thought of changing your image? If not, it's something you might want to consider. I remember about ten years ago, when I was a naive young kid in my early twenties. I was very frustrated because I wasn't meeting any girls and I couldn't figure out why. At first I thought it must be because of the crowd I hung around with. After all, it couldn't possibly have been my fault, right? It had to be my friends. Yeah, that was it. Those nerds were killing my social life.

That was the only possible explanation. All I needed was to find a new bunch of friends, and all my problems would be solved. But the more I thought about it, the more I realized that my friends were not to blame for my misfortunes. Maybe it was the way I looked. I decided the thing I needed was a complete change of image.

After all, if there's one thing Hollywood has taught us, it's that the only thing any guy needs to turn from a loser into a winner is a) a new car, b) a new wardrobe, and c) a new hairstyle! I decided to go for the trifecta. The Triple Crown of Image Alteration!

The first thing I did was get a new haircut. At the time, the popular look was a military-style cut similar to the one Arnold Schwarzenegger had in the movie *Commando*. So I got one of those; I even used gel to make my hair stand up and look spiky.

Then I bought a new wardrobe. It was the first time in my life I went out and bought some of my own clothes, instead of just endlessly recycling the clothes my Mom gave me at Christmas every year.

Then I bought a hot red sports car—an '83 Firebird. Now I was all set. I had everything I needed (well, everything except my own swingin' bachelor pad, but when you've got a sportin' roadster like mine, it's like having a motel on wheels, right?) Then I started working out, getting in shape, building up my muscles. This, I figured, would only make me more irresistable to the chicks. After several months of weightlifting, I was ready. Bring on the girls!

Well, needless to say, I didn't get any girls right away, but at least I looked good! My new, improved looks gave me the confidence to approach more girls, which eventually led to my improving my social status, big time.

Looking your best just may give you the edge you need over the competition. Let's say a girl has a choice between you and one other guy. The other guy is wearing nicely polished shoes, a sportcoat, dress slacks, a tie, and is well-groomed. You're wearing a baseball cap, a t-shirt that reads "Just Do Me," ripped jeans, and an old pair of sneakers. Who do you think the girl is more likely to go for?

How you dress really does say something about who you are as a person. Whether you like it or not, many people are prone to judge you based on your appearance. A lot of Shy Guys will go out in public wearing rock concert t-shirts, or the grungy, paint-stained sweatpants they wear when they fix stuff up around the house. That outfit is not going to impress anyone.

Shy Guys are often hopelessly out of date when it comes to fashion. Here's a little hint for you, though: if you're still wearing two-tone pants, go shopping. Here's another one: stone-washed jeans went out with the eighties.

Because Shy Guys spend so much of their time indoors, fashion trends may come and go before the Shy Guy is even aware of them. I must confess, as a writer who works at home, I find myself playing fashion victim from time to time. For instance, I always wore my tube socks all the way up to my knees, which was the style back in the day. It wasn't until I was at a party and a girl came over and yanked my socks down to my ankles that I realized that times had changed.

Sometimes Shy Guys must be violently dragged into new fashion eras. I must confess to having a sentimental attachment to my 1980s parachute pants that lasted long after their fashion statement had expired. But they were just so damned comfortable!

As you can see, it's not easy keeping up with trends. Your best bet is to find somebody who is fashionable (either someone you know or a celebrity) and study what they wear. Duplicate the things you like, only in different colors. If you're going the celebrity route, I'd avoid the Michael Jackson look. Make sure you pick someone who is at the peak of their popularity.

If you have a sister, or a female friend, ask her for fashion advice. If possible, take her shopping with you and have her help you pick out clothes. Girls tend to follow fashion much more closely than guys do, and their advice can be invaluable. You may want to subscribe to a men's fashion magazine, like *GQ*, or at least occasionally flip through an issue to pick up some ideas. Another suggestion: If you wear glasses, have you ever considered switching to contact lenses? If you've got a lot of money, you may even want to consider laser surgery to correct your vision permanently. (It costs about $4,000.)

I prefer to have female stylists cut my hair, because I figure girls know what other girls like, and can help you pick the look that they will find most attractive. And if your hairdresser is a babe, who knows where that could lead? If you are still going to the same barber you went to as a kid, getting that same $8 haircut, it may be time for a change.

As far as cars go, it's probably not that important what you drive, as long as it's not an embarrassment. You're not going to score any points with a girl if your car breaks down on the way to pick her up for your first date! A nice car does make a good impression. Even if you have to borrow a car from your friend or your parents, that's fine. Just make up some story about your own car being in the shop.

Ultimately, of course, you want your girl to love you for who you are, not the way you dress or the kind of car you drive. But until such a time as you actually get a girlfriend, it couldn't hurt to be a little image-conscious. Pay attention to the situations that require a collar, shoes, or even a jacket and tie.

Another thing you may wish to consider is exercise. If you don't already do it, a steady routine of working out can do wonders for your self-esteem. You can build your body and your confidence at the same time. Not only that, but you'll live longer. Exercise can be frustrating when results don't come quickly, but stick with it. It will take at least a month before you begin to notice any change in your physique. Once you get yourself in shape and have a body you can be proud of, you'll feel better about yourself. After you've been working out for a while, you'll be convinced that you can have any girl in the world.

If weightlifting is not your thing, you may want to consider jogging or brisk walking. The important thing is to make yourself as attractive as possible to the ladies out there. A lot of gals do aerobics, fix their hair up, and put on makeup. The least you can do in return is not let yourself go. If all you're doing is the twelve-ounce curl, and making your beer gut bigger, you're going to grow disgusted with your own appearance, and then nobody will love you—not even you!

You don't have to be obsessive about it. Lift weights three times a week for forty minutes at a stretch, and try to get a half-hour a day of aerobic exercise. Also, watch your diet. Try not to overeat. The better you look, the better-looking the females you have access to will be.

There are no guarantees that any of this stuff will work. But it couldn't hurt to make yourself as presentable as possible. If you are at all uncomfortable with your appearance, as many Shy Guys are, it could be a serious drawback that prevents you from meeting anyone. But once you are satisfied with the way you look, you may find the confidence you need to succeed.

There's one other thing I'd like to mention. Just because you're not the best-looking guy in the world, don't let that hold you back. Good looks do not necessarily guarantee you will get girls. Don't be discouraged just because you don't look like Brad Pitt. Good-looking guys have problems hooking up, too. If a girl thinks you are a smooth Casanova, she will want nothing to do with you. She doesn't want to be your latest conquest. If your come-on seems a little too slick, too refined, you may wind up blowing the whole thing.

Sometimes I think you're almost better off if you're only average-looking! When a handsome stud approaches them, girls automatically assume he has a girlfriend, and, if he doesn't, there must be something wrong with him. Average-looking guys do not have to face this problem. Often girls are distrustful of good-looking guys. Their assumption is that a handsome guy can have any girl he wants, so he must play the field a lot. Ironically, it is this very type of thinking that prevents handsome guys from playing the field.

So if you're not a superstud, don't worry about it. Superstuds have problems hooking up, too, just the same as the regular folks.

Chapter Twelve

The Shy Guy in the LTR (Long-term Relationship)

Up to now, the focus of this book has been on overcoming your fear of rejection, and learning how to score with girls. These are the two areas where Shy Guys generally need the most work. Once you enter into a steady relationship with a girl, your shyness with her evaporates. Because you are comfortable around her, you can say whatever you need to say. I've seen Shy Guys display phenomenal amounts of confidence with their girlfriends once they entered into LTRs with them.

I've even worked out a mathematical formula to explain this phenomenom. It looks like this: Steady Sex = Confidence. But there may be some Shy Guys who need some help in entering and maintaining a Long-term Relationship. I don't claim to be an expert on LTRs, but I'll do the best I can.

Okay, so you've had the first date. Where do you go from here? If you and the girl really hit it off, you'll probably be on the phone with each other the next day, and every day thereafter, seeing each other every chance you get. If you're not head over heels for each other, you'll want to take things a little bit slower. Don't call her every day—not right off the bat. Remember what Damone said in *Fast Times*: Don't let on how much you like her. A good rule of thumb is to plan your next date for a week or so after the first one.

In my younger, more impetuous days, I used to get so excited about the prospect of getting laid that I would meet a new girl, and want to go out with her two or three times that week. This generally gave the girl the impression that I was really interested in her, when really, I was just interested in sex.

A girl I was dating came over one time and I lustily started smooching her. Surprised by my enthusiasm, she remarked, "Wow, you must have really missed me!" She was wrong. I missed the sex.

But that was in my wild youth, when I wasn't after a real relationship. These days, I know that slow and steady is the way to go. You want to take your time when beginning a new relationship. You don't want to rush into anything. If something is meant to happen, it will happen. Be patient. Let things proceed at their own pace.

Gradually, if you and your girl are meant to be together, everything will fall into place. You will meet her family and friends, she will meet yours. You will become aware of each other's little quirks and eccentricities. Once you start speaking to each other every night on the phone, you know things are getting serious. When she starts calling you several times a day, even at work, you know the girl is in love.

The secret of any successful relationship is compromise. This can be a difficult adjustment for Shy Guys, who have spent most of their lives alone and are resistant to change. A Shy Guy is accustomed to being able to do whatever he wants. He can sit around the house in his underwear, leave dirty dishes in the sink, leave clothes on the floor.

When you enter into a LTR, all of that changes. Suddenly, you can't just be thinking of yourself anymore. You've got to put the toilet seat down every now and then. You've got to put the relationship first. If you are not willing to compromise, your relationships will not last very long. Entering into a Long-term Relationship means leaving those old selfish habits behind. You've got to be thinking of what's best for the two of you, as a unit.

Of course, most Shy Guys still need their time alone. It is important to communicate this to your girl, that you have a strong need for some private time away, even from her. From time to time, you may have to tell your girl, "Honey, I need to get some reading done." Don't be afraid to express your need for a little time alone every now and then. It's like that Chicago song says, "Everybody needs a little time away, far away from the one they love."

If she respects you as a person, she will grant your wish. Just because you want some time away from her does not mean that you care about her any less; it just means that you have your own needs, outside of the relationship, that need tending, as well. You had a whole life before she came along. You can't be expected to turn your back on your old life completely!

The main thing is that you are both equally willing to compromise. If she is willing to make sacrifices for you, you should be prepared to do the same for her. No one partner should be giving more than the other. If a relationship is to work, it must be an equal partnership.

Most compromises are pretty easy to reach, with only a little bit of effort from each person. One night, you watch a baseball game together on TV. The next night, you watch one of her crappy soap operas. One week, you bring her to a Jackie Chan action flick. The next week, she drags you to a chick flick. One week, she drags you to a flea market. The next week, you take her to a Demolition Derby. I know one guy whose wife dragged him to a doll convention! Sheesh! Talk about making sacrifices!

Some couples find it simplest to do some things separately, such as having TVs in different rooms. If she wants a Girls' Night Out, let her go; in exchange, she should grant you a night out with the boys every now and then. You don't have to do everything together. You each had lives of your own before you entered the relationship. Why should either of you sacrifice your individuality now? You are not the same person as your girlfriend; you have different interests, likes, and dislikes. It would be foolish to think you enjoy all of the same things.

Some people find they are unable to sleep with another person—even a lover—in their bed. So, after sex, they go to separate rooms. Don't be shy about telling your lover that after the sex and the cuddling are over, the only way you can sleep is in your own bed. If she really loves you, she will understand. There is a radical new theory among loving couples that two human beings are not meant to share one bed. Part of being in a relationship is knowing that you don't have to spend every moment together.

After Compromise, the most important traits of a good relationship are as follows: Communication, Commitment, and Common Interests. I call them the Four Cs of Relationships. You can also add Compatibility and Compassion, if you want to stretch a point.

As the movie *About Last Night . . .* has shown us, the guy should never be the first one to say "I love you." The girl should always say it first. This way, you don't embarrass yourself if she doesn't say it back. A Shy Guy does not want to say or do anything unless he is certain his girl feels exactly the same way he does.

Once you have entered into a Long-term Relationship, there is a tendency for guys to slack off a little bit in the romance department. Girls like it when you keep romancing them as you did in the beginning. They love to receive flowers, and not just on Valentine's Day. They love it when you go out of your way to do something for them, instead of just doing things on holidays because you feel you have to. She shouldn't have to call you all the time. You can pick up the phone and call her sometimes, too.

One thing a lot of couples like to do to for fun is plan a getaway weekend together. There are a million places you can go—the beach, the mountains, a ski resort, a theme park, whatever. Some of them don't cost too much. Many couples enjoy spending a weekend at a bed and breakfast.

You'll probably want to take a few minivacations with your girl before you go for the big one- or two-week vacation. That's a lot of time for two people to spend together. You'd better see how well you get along for a weekend before you do anything drastic. Because that first long vacation together is a pretty serious step, my friend!

After several months of dating, you and your girl may decide to move in together. This usually starts slowly. First, she keeps a spare toothbrush at your house. Then a change of underwear. Then some makeup. Maybe some feminine protection stuff you don't even want to know about.

Gradually, you come to realize it doesn't make sense for her to divide her stuff between two apartments, and you ask her to move in. There are many benefits to this move—chief among them that it cuts all your living expenses in half! As wonderful as it is to be in a steady relationship, it's even more satisfying to be able to divide all your monthly bills in two.

The most successful relationships are the ones in which the couples don't isolate themselves from the world around them. A healthy relationship is one where you spend half the time with your lover, and the other half with your friends, family, and co-workers. In this way, you are a whole person and your girl is a whole person. You are both more well-rounded and have more to talk about.

You may even choose to include your friends in some of your social outings with your girlfriend, if you are doing something nonromantic, like seeing a concert or a sporting event. It is also healthy to get together with other couples from time to time, for dinner or coffee. You can compare notes with them, and maybe pick up some tips that will improve your own relationship.

One of the most important things to remember when you start a new relationship is not to blow your friends off. Many guys (and girls) are guilty of abandoning their friends whenever they get a new lover, only to come crawling back like a friendship-hungry dog when the relationship goes sour.

No one wants to be a friend of convenience. Your friends were always there for you when you were single. Suddenly, now that you're in a relationship, it is easy to start taking them for granted. Girls tend to be guilty of this type of behavior more than guys, but I've seen guys do it, too. Friends strongly resent it when you turn your back on them to enter a new romance. There is an assumption some people make that their friends will always be there when their relationship crumbles. Don't count on it. One day, you may come out of a failed romance and find that all your friends are gone. Relationships will come and go, but a good friend is one that lasts forever, as long as you don't abuse the friendship. Treat your friends right, and they will always be there for you.

I think the reason for the Abandoned Friends Syndrome is simple. When you are younger, your friends are all you have. They are your support group, your social circle, your safety net. You do not yet possess the skills to start dating. Once you acquire those skills, and begin having a social life, you are no longer dependent on your friends to provide a social outlet, so you cut them loose. You have no further need for them, or so you think.

This is the mark of someone who does not place a very high value on friendship. If your friends are nothing more than simple props to occupy your time until you get a girlfriend, then you are obviously not a very good friend.

A well-rounded guy is one who places an equal emphasis on both friendship and romance. Your girlfriend will respect you more if she sees you treating your friends with the same respect you treat her with. She will consider you a thoughtful, considerate person. It is often interesting for a girl to see how you behave around your friends, because she is seeing a side of you which you don't display around her. In this way, she gets a much better overall picture of who you are.

Of course, there is always the danger of going too far overboard in the friendship department. Don't devote more time to your friends than you do to your girlfriend, and don't invite your friends to come with you on all your dates. One of the biggest complaints any girl has is, "You spend way too much time with your friends!" Try to find the right balance between time spent with your buddies and time spent with your lady. It can be difficult, but with proper planning, it can be done. Obviously, your girlfriend should always receive the greater amount of attention. (Your friends may have been there first, but your girlfriend is the one you're sleeping with! You've got to keep those priorities straight!)

The other big complaint girls have about guys is, "You never talk to me! You never tell me about your feelings!" The best way for a Shy Guy to succeed in a relationship is by opening up to his girl.

Guys tend not to be as emotional as girls. Guys tend to be

more analytical. When a girl asks you what you're feeling, the truth of the matter is that most of the time, you're not feeling anything. You're analyzing a problem, and planning what steps you can take to fix it. If you ever are feeling anything, you should make your girl aware of this rare event. Whenever the stray feeling does cross your mind, throw her a bone and let her know about it. It will mean a lot to her.

Guys usually feel it is not necessary to express their feelings to a girl, that their simple presence in a relationship is enough. If a girl says, "You never tell me you love me," a guy will respond, "Hey, I'm here, aren't I?" A guy thinks that simply by showing up and spending time with a girl, he has done his part. But this is never enough.

Girls always want you to tell them how important they are to you. They want to hear how much you love them. They want you to send them flowers and do nice things for them. It's not enough to simply show up. Often guys think they are in a very satisfying, healthy relationship; meanwhile, the woman is down at her lawyer's office filling out divorce papers. Because guys are not as accustomed to talking about their feelings, girlfriends can feel abandoned and alone. Many times, guys really are clueless, and never see the breakup coming.

If you express your emotions to your girl, at least there is the possibility of avoiding that breakup before it hits you from out of nowhere like a freight train. I recommend a policy of near-total honesty for Shy Guys in relationships. Tell her almost everything. You'll feel better about yourself, and she'll love you for it.

The reason I don't endorse total honesty is because there are some things your girl doesn't need to know about that might hurt her feelings. If your friends dragged you to a nudie bar for a bachelor party, she doesn't need to hear about that. If you've just been assigned to work with a gorgeous girl in your office, keep it to yourself. If your girl cooks a dish that you can't stand, just pretend to chew it and spit it out in your napkin or feed it to the cat under the table. If you ran into an ex-girlfriend and she kissed you, don't share it. If you think your girl's new haircut looks stupid, keep it to yourself. Even though total honesty sounds like a good idea in theory, it really is not. There are little lies every member of a couple tells the other every day. Very few relationships could survive total honesty. (Just look how much trouble Jim Carrey got in when he had to tell the whole truth for one day in *Liar, Liar*!)

One area in which you should try total honesty is when it comes to being faithful. Many years ago, filmmaker George Lucas, of *Star Wars* fame, made a pact with his wife. They promised each other that if either one of them ever cheated on the other, they would disclose it. Because neither of them could bear the thought of telling the other, neither one ever cheated. This sounds like a wise approach to me.

Some say that one of the most important parts of any relationship is forgiveness. Many is the relationship that has been saved, perhaps even strengthened, after one of the partners confessed an infidelity. Your own levels of forgiveness may vary. I tend to go with the ancient theory that once you lose the trust in a relationship, you've lost everything.

Girls can be very sensitive, so you really have to be careful what you say to them. They are famous for misinterpreting remarks that you thought were harmless. It's amazing how many times you are trying to compliment a girl and she gets insulted instead. Guys and girls speak a different language. Most of this stuff has been said in other books. I'm just condensing it for you.

Another thing I'd like to point out is that guys tend to be very absent-minded when it comes to certain things. We don't always remember birthdays or anniversaries, and we sometimes forget to do certain chores we said we would do. That's just the way guys are. We prioritize. We like to concentrate on one thing at a time. If we are working on a big project at the office, we may forget that tonight is the big dinner party we promised we would go to.

Girls just have to be forgiving when it comes to guys' memory lapses. We don't have them on purpose. It's just that our brains only retain the important information, like sports statistics, dialogue from movies and TV shows, and dirty jokes.

The best relationships are those in which the couple has a lot in common, and compatible personalities. The more things you have in common, the more time you can spend together. The more compatible your personalities, the more you will enjoy talking to each other. Ideally, your lover should also be your best friend. That's a nice dream. I'm not sure how often it really happens, but, at the very least, you should share some interests.

It helps to be willing to try something that your partner is into. For instance, my buddy John got his girlfriend, Janet, hooked on his hobby of bird-watching. Now it is something they can enjoy together.

If you are constantly forcing your lover to do things that she does not really enjoy, this could lead to disharmony. Do not devote more time to your hobby than you do to your girl. Many a relationship has been ruined by a man's obsession with sports or cars. Guys tend to get far more obsessed with things than girls do. That's just the way guys are. Whatever you're into—be it taxidermy or model airplanes—make sure you devote as much time to your girl as you do to whatever hobbies you have.

It's best to have as many things in common as possible. If you are a fast walker, you may not want to date a slow walker. If you like the room temperature cold all the time, you may have some conflicts with a girl who likes it warm all the time. These are minor points, really, and they may seem trivial to some, but they are things you may wish to consider when deciding whether or not you want to spend the rest of your life with someone.

One thing I'd like to mention here is that some degree of arguing is healthy in any relationship. If there is something bothering you, get it out in the open. If you keep things inside, it will only make things worse in the long run. Shy Guys have a tendency to avoid conflict whenever possible. The Shy Guy feels it is best to keep bad feelings inside, save them up for a long time, and then go on a shooting spree at the post office.

If there is something bothering you, let your girl know. Maybe it is something that can be easily fixed. Encourage your girl to be open about things that bother her. You've got to keep the lines of communication open. (Oops I'm straying dangerously close to John Gray territory here! I'd better lay off the psychology and stick to what I know best—making pop culture analogies!)

It's like Billy Joel says in his song, "Tell Her About It": If there is something you are feeling—any thought, any emotion, any hope or dream—you've got to tell your woman about it. Only when you do this can she give you unconditional love.

If you think B. J. doesn't know what he's talking about, let me just remind you of one thing: he got Christie Brinkley! Okay, so they got divorced, but still, any guy who lands a supermodel—especially a guy who looks like Billy Joel—is definitely worth listening to!

There are several different types of couples that I'd like to talk about. The first type is the Combative Couple, the one that argues about everything. George's parents on *Seinfeld* are a good example of a Combative Couple. If they didn't fight all the time, they would have absolutely nothing to talk about. They thrive on confrontation. The constant flow of negative energy directed at each other is what keeps the relationship going.

The second type is the Content Couple, the one that gets along pretty well, with only the occasional disagreement. Generally, the Content Couple will gently mock each other's driving ability ("You tailgate too much! You drive too fast!"), but that's about as serious as their fights get. I'd say most couples fall into this category. Their relationship has its ups and downs, but most of the time, they maintain an even keel.

Then we have the Lovey-Dovey Couple, who call each other cute pet names and can't keep their hands off each other. This is the couple that is most hated above all others. Nobody can stand a Lovey-Dovey Couple—not single people, not other couples. Everybody hates them. If you can't imagine why, then you've never had to endure an entire night of two grown-ups talking baby talk to each other all night.

You don't ever want to be part of a Lovey-Dovey Couple, because if you are, then everyone will hate you. A good warning sign that you have crossed the line is if you start calling your girlfriend, "Shmoopie."

Finally, we have the Abusive Couple, which is one step beyond the Combative Couple. This is a couple that is probably not meant to be together. A sample conversation sounds something like this, "I hate you!" "I hate you, too!" "I'll kill you!" "You suck in bed!" I would certainly hope that no one reading this book ever enters into a relationship like that. It's just not healthy.

If you are in a relationship that is not going well, don't be too shy to end it. Most Shy Guys would rather die than to face the confrontation of ending a relationship, but there are times when it must be done.

I know one Shy Guy who uses the Passive/Aggressive approach to break up with his girlfriends. First, he starts calling them less often. The phone calls become shorter and shorter. Then he becomes cold and distant on dates. He gradually shows less and less interest in the girl, both physically and mentally. Finally, the girl senses something is wrong, and she breaks up with him. Thus, my friend is spared the trouble of having to initiate the breakup himself.

I think a better approach is to address the situation head-on. The longer you let it wait, the worse it's going to get. Since this book isn't called The Coward's Guide to Ending Relationships, you may want to actually confront your girl with (shudder) the truth! Explain to her honestly the problems you have with the relationship. Talk your problems through. Who knows? Maybe they can be resolved.

But if they can't be, stand firm on your decision. Any problems you have with a relationship will only become more bothersome to you as time goes on. Those problems will always stand in the way of your happiness. It doesn't help either one of you to stay in an unhealthy relationship.

Just as one must overcome shyness to meet a girl, sometimes one must overcome shyness to let her go.

In the first half of this chapter, we discussed male/female relationships that are based on a mutual love. In the second half, I want to talk about a type of long-term relationship that Shy Guys often find themselves in that is far less satisfying.

"Just Good Friends"

Men and women cannot be friends.
—Billy Crystal
When Harry Met Sally . . .

This rather cynical quote is not entirely true, but in the case of most Shy Guys, it usually is. As the movie notes, the sex thing always gets in the way. As the screenwriter of *When Harry Met Sally . . .* smartly observes, whenever a man and a woman become friends, one of the two is usually romantically interested in the other. Interestingly enough, the movie was written by a woman, Nora Ephron, and the whole movie seems to play into this idea that any friendship between a man and a woman is only a prelude to romance. Another movie, 1996's *Phat Beach*, dealt with a similar situation, but used street terminology to explain it. According to one of the characters in that hip-hop comedy, "A friend is just a girl that you haven't fucked yet!"

Many girls fantasize about being friends with a guy first, and then becoming lovers. Supposedly the best relationships start off this way. Well, let me state here and now that no guy in the history of the world has ever wanted to start off being just friends with a girl and then becoming lovers. Guys just don't think that way. We want to start off with sex, and let a relationship grow from there.

Most Shy Guys I know are, as noted before, hopeless romantics, who believe in love at first sight, rescuing damsels in distress, happy endings, and all that good stuff. The problem is that Shy Guys often find themselves platonic friends with a girl, when what they really want is a relationship. Every Shy Guy, at one time or another, has heard the most dreaded expression a girl can utter: "I like you as a friend." Another popular phrase often heard by Shy Guys is, "I think of you as a brother." Both these phrases essentially mean the same thing: "I have absolutely no attraction to you whatsoever." Or, to put it another way, "I don't think of you as having a penis."

This is a very common situation for Shy Guys, who, because of cowardice/weakness, will often settle for being friends with a girl when they would much prefer to have her as a lover. A Shy Guy figures that if he told a girl how he really feels, he might lose her altogether. If he hangs in there as a friend, he might still have a chance. So most Shy Guys play it safe, and keep their feelings to themselves.

I know a lot of guys who've had female friends, always secretly hoping it would lead to something more. The girl is often completely clueless, never suspecting that her "best friend" is actually hoping to sleep with her. Imagine how shocked the girls of the world would be if they knew that most of the guys they consider their friends are actually hoping to someday have sex with them!

Most Shy Guys operate under the delusion that if they wait around long enough, eventually the girl who is a friend will become a girlfriend. Every Shy Guy tricks himself into thinking, "Someday, there'll come a day when she breaks up with her boyfriend . . . when she comes crying into my arms . . . and then she'll be mine! Either that or one night, she'll get so drunk that I'll be able to take advantage of her!"

Most Shy Guys are so insecure about expressing their true feelings for a girl that they'll concoct elaborate fantasies about how to win her over. Unfortunately, those fantasies are just that, and, in most cases, will never be anything more than that. Chances are, if the girl ever does break up with her boyfriend, she will have another guy, not you, waiting to take his place. And no matter how drunk she gets, she still won't have sex with you. If she wasn't attracted to you sober, liquor isn't going to change that.

Often, a girl will let a Shy Guy sleep in her bed. After all, she thinks of you as some harmless, dickless, nonsexual friend. These nights are the most frustrating of all for a Shy Guy. Imagine that the girl of your dreams has finally consented to let you spend the night in her bed—as long as you don't lay a finger on her. That's the kind of thing that could drive a guy into therapy.

Let me give you a real-life example. The names have been changed to protect my fellow Shy Guys.

A friend of mine—we'll call him Joey Jo-Jo Jr. Shabbadoo—knew this girl named Laura, who he met in college. Laura loved to be around Joey. They spent all their time together. Nobody could make Laura laugh like Joey could. Laura loved having Joey as a friend, but she had absolutely no romantic interest in him. She just wasn't attracted to him sexually. Joey used to occasionally spend the night in Laura's apartment, sleeping beside her, never touching her. Joey was strongly attracted to Laura. In fact, he was in love with her. But no matter what he did, he couldn't get Laura to love him the way he wanted her to.

The situation used to drive Joey crazy. He was flattered by the attention Laura gave him. She laughed at all his jokes, and she loved doing the same things he did. Joey figured if he just hung in there long enough, eventually he would win her over. But it just didn't happen. Joey got so frustrated by the situation, that, one night, he banged his head through the wall in his kitchen. That hole is still there to this day, a painful reminder of a love unconsummated.

Joey used to come home from Laura's house every night and play the Neil Young song "Only Love Can Break Your Heart." To this day, Joey cannot hear that song without thinking of the anguish that Laura put him through—all of it unintentional, by the way. While Joey was sinking as low as he could go, Laura was having a great time hanging out with her good friend.

Finally, Joey reached his breaking point. One night, he put his heart on the line, telling Laura how he really felt about her, how attracted to her he was. He ended by saying, "I cannot spend one more platonic night in this apartment!" With that, he walked out of her life.

Needless to say, he never saw her again. He had just spent six months investing in a one-sided relationship, and he couldn't take it any more. He had made his stand. He had said his piece, and, even though he didn't get what he wanted, at least he now had peace of mind. This horribly one-sided relationship had finally come to an end.

Too bad it took him six months to do it.

Another example: Another buddy of mine, Dan, was working in a law firm and had become pretty good friends with one of the secretaries, Lisa. Lisa had a steady boyfriend (a deadbeat, of course), but she enjoyed hanging out with Dan. Lisa's boyfriend was a rock 'n' roller; Dan was the polar opposite—a clean-cut nice guy. But still, Lisa enjoyed her time with Dan. Dan and Lisa went to concerts, ate lunch together every day, went out clubbing at night.

From time to time, Lisa would tell Dan about her lowlife boyfriend, and Dan made a promise to himself that he would save her from this villain. Many Shy Guys see themselves as knights in shining armor who will rescue damsels in distress from their evil boyfriends. Sadly, it only works that way in the movies. In real life, girls often stay in abusive relationships, even though they've got a nice guy waiting on the sidelines. The sad fact of the matter is that some girls are attracted to scumbags.

A nice guy doesn't stand a chance with a girl like this. She only wants a guy who's going to neglect her, mistreat her, and walk all over her. When you show up with flowers in hand, offering to open her car door for her, well forget it, pal. This girl wants nothing to do with you.

My friend Dan found this out the hard way. He started taking guitar lessons, in an effort to be the kind of guy Lisa goes for. No matter much we tried to convince Dan not to waste his time on Lisa, he wouldn't listen. One night, Dan actually had a chance of consummating his relationship with Lisa when the two of them got drunk in her apartment. But Dan was too drunk to do anything but pass out.

Eventually, Dan couldn't handle being "just good friends" with Lisa, and he told her he didn't want to see her anymore.

With tears in her eyes, Lisa responded, "I feel like I just lost my best friend." But Dan stood his ground, and stopped spending time with her outside of work. He could have continued the relationship as it was, platonically, but he didn't want to put himself through that kind of hell anymore. He couldn't stand the frustration of being so close to her, yet unable to act on his desires.

It was far healthier for Dan to just end the relationship completely.

After reading this chapter, you may think I subscribe to the *When Harry Met Sally . . .* notion that guys and girls cannot be friends. The truth is, I think guys and gals *can* be friends, as long as neither of the two has any physical attraction to the other. I've seen examples of successful guy/girl friendships, and in every case, the guy and the girl have absolutely no sexual interest in each other. I think it's healthy for every guy—especially Shy Guys—to have girls in their lives, whether as friends or lovers.

But—and this is a big but—only as long as they're doing it for the right reasons. If you have befriended a girl because you are waiting for the opportunity to get down her pants, you're wasting your time. If you have pursued her friendship because you enjoy her company, then by all means, go for it. I've just seen too many guys go for the "Just Good Friends" option in the futile hope that it could someday lead to true love. That approach only leads to heartbreak. It is a road better left untaken. Following that route will only cause you sleepless nights, misery, and frustration.

So the next time your dream girl offers to be platonic friends with you, just tell her this: "I ain't Plato!"

Chapter Thirteen 

Are You Ready to Get Married?

I've got a problem here. My editor has asked me to write a chapter on marriage. The thing is, I'm single. Although I am ready to get married, I am missing that one crucial thing—namely, a fiancée. So I can't write about marriage from a firsthand perspective.

Over the years, I've encountered just about every type of dating situation you could think of: Long-term Relationships, Short-term Relationships, Long-distance Relationships, Fatal Attractions (I've been both the victim and the aggressor), Blind Dates, Double Dates (almost always disasters, in my case; that other couple always throws off my rhythm), One-sided Relationships (again, some where I had hand, some where the girl had hand)—the list is a lengthy one.

I first started dating at the age of nineteen. I've been doing this for fourteen years now. I'd say dating is one subject I know better than most people. But marriage? That's a whole different can of worms. I can't claim to be an authority on that. And I'm not sure a Shy Guy really needs much coaching in this department.

Let's face it: most Shy Guys, once they get a girl, will probably stick with her until they walk down the aisle together. It is not in the nature of a Shy Guy to play the field.

I think it's time to call in somebody who knows this topic far better than I—that's right, my old pal, Charlie! Okay, let's ask Charlie the big question: How do you know when you're ready to get married?

"You start feeling content. You have a deep sense of security, as opposed to the intense feelings that you experience at the beginning of a relationship. The relationship is always comfortable. You really know each other.

"Before you get married, you should talk through all the different things that can come up, things like sex, money, and housework. Ask yourselves, do you want the same things out of life? Do you have the same goals and values?

"Try to identify potential problems, and how they can be solved. For instance, my own girlfriend has a cat that likes to piss on the carpet, and that's an issue that had to be resolved before we get married. Figure out things like this that could build long-term resentment. The more you talk about things, the better. You should be able to talk about any issue. Don't hide anything major.

"Try to determine your compatibility. By that, I am referring to common interests. Establish that you have more in common than not in common, or the relationship will not work."

Thanks, Charlie! I knew you'd come through for me. I hope you were all able to get something out of that.

Now, let's say you've overcome your shyness enough to have attained the Shy Guy's Holy Grail, a real, live girlfriend. Let's say you love her and she loves you. Maybe the two of you have even moved in together.

Now you're ready to take that final step: Marriage! Or are you? Maybe you're really not ready to settle down yet. Maybe you still have a few more wild oats to sow. Speaking from a personal standpoint, I know that since I didn't date for the first eighteen years of my life, I had a lot of lost time to make up for. You may feel the same way. Every year that you're single while going through puberty feels like a thousand years! That's a memory that never fades.

Make sure you've got all your single yearnings out of the way before you propose to anyone. Have you accomplished everything you had hoped to as a single guy? If so, you might be ready to tie the knot. Or maybe not.

Take the following quiz, and see if you really are in a matrimonial mood.

1) Are you ready to spend the rest of your life with one woman?
2) Have you discussed the prospect of having children with your girlfriend? More than one relationship has ended because the partners disagreed on how many kids to have, if any.
3) Are there any problems that would prevent your girl from marrying you (i.e., she's not old enough, her parents would object, you have religious differences, you have sexual problems, etc.)?
4) Do you have any doubts? If so, you may wish to reconsider.
5) Do you love her? I mean, really love her? No, I mean, really.
6) Is she your best friend, as well as your lover? This is kind of essential. If you're going to spend the rest of

your life with someone, you'd better get along pretty well with her!

7) Do you feel mature enough to handle the responsibilities of marriage?
8) Are you able to talk your problems through to a mutually satisfying resolution?
9) Do you ever run out of things to talk about with her?
10) Do you share a lot of common interests?
11) Do you feel you can be faithful to her?
12) Why isn't this chapter funny? Where are the movie and TV references?
13) Are you prepared to take out the garbage twice a week for the rest of your life?
14) If the author knows so much about marriage, why isn't he married yet?
15) Are you certain that your girl is going to say "yes" if you ask her? If you're not 100 percent sure, *don't ask her*! That's just not the way it's done. Generally, most couples talk about marriage for years before they actually do it. As a rule, couples seem to date for two to five years before getting married.
16) Do you want a big wedding, or do you want to run off to Vegas and get married by an Elvis impersonator? (I'm rather partial to the Elvis scenario, myself. Weddings are so expensive. You could use that money to put a down payment on a house, instead.)
17) How come this so-called quiz doesn't have funny multiple-choice answers, like the one at the beginning of the book? Because it's not that kind of quiz! Marriage is serious business, and intended to be dealt with in a serious manner! This is a lifetime commitment we're talking about!

18) How do you know if someone is the right girl for you? When it's right, you just know.
19) What does getting married have to do with being shy? Nothing, really!
20) What happens if my friends get me a hooker at my bachelor party? Stay away from her! She probably has AIDS!
21) How well do you get along with her family? Remember, you're not just marrying your girlfriend. You're also marrying every member of her family, all of her friends, and every person she knows!
22) Do you agree with her on where you would like to live?
23) Does she have any pets with bad habits—like pissing on the carpet?
24) Does she have any bizarre psychological hang-ups that could cause problems further down the line?
25) If marriage is so great, how come Larry King has been married six times? I'm not sure. That's something you'd have to ask Larry. Maybe he's using "Will you marry me?" as his pickup line.

One thing I'd like to mention here is that if you have been dating a girl for a few years, and you haven't proposed to her yet, she may begin to get what I call the "Five-Year Itch." This is when your girl gives you an ultimatum: Show me the engagement ring or hit the road! I know more than one guy who was inspired to pop the question after being given the "shit or get off the pot" speech. My old pal Dave Polito has a theory that the happiest time in any guy's life are the years when he's dating his girlfriend, without the burden of being married to her. As the old saying goes, why should you buy the cow when you can get the milk for free?

Dave's theory is that no guy ever wants the courtship to end, because it is the last time in any guy's life he will have no obligations and no commitments. It is the last time in his life he will know true freedom. I don't agree with Dave on this point, but I can certainly see his logic. I'm kind of old-fashioned, and I see marriage as the logical next step in a healthy relationship. It's sort of a culmination of years of dating. It's a celebration, as it were, an affirmation of the strength and the success of the union.

Being part of a healthy marriage makes you a more complete person, and it gives you a happier, more well-rounded life. A successful marriage is a goal that you and your woman can work together at achieving for the rest of your lives. Having a spouse who supports you, encourages you, and gives you steady sex takes a lot of the stress and worry out of life. If all goes well, it could be the best thing that ever happened to you.

Just make sure you're ready for it when the time comes. There are no answers to the above quiz, except for answers that you choose to give.

From this point on, you're on your own.

Epilogue

So What Have We Learned?

So we've come to the end of our little self-help book. By this time, you're probably saying to yourself, "Hey, this guy has got some great ideas! I can't wait to go out and try out some of his suggestions!" Either that, or you're saying, "What a rip-off! I read this whole book, and I'm just as shy as I was when I started! I want my money back!"

Which reaction you have depends a lot on what you choose to do with the information I've given you. If you choose to ignore all of my suggestions, you'll probably go on being as shy as you always have been. But if you actually follow some of my advice, and try to put it into practice, you may find it works as well for you as it has for me. (If it were possible for me to go back in time and give myself a copy of this book, I would have been married ten years ago!)

I wish I could wave a magic wand and cure all the shy people in the world, but that's just not possible. If you really want it to happen, you have to do it yourself. Buying this book was a good start. It shows you have a healthy interest in overcoming this affliction. Shyness has held you back your whole life; it's always been an obstacle. Maybe it's time you got over it and started really living.

If you were born with the shyness gene, as I was, chances are you'll have it your entire life. But just because you are shy doesn't mean you can't get out there and meet girls. I have to agree with Rocky Balboa, who says in our preface: "A lot of people think shyness is a disease. But I think it's all right." There's nothing wrong with being shy, as long as you don't let it hold you back.

Recently I was talking to a couple of Shy Guys. I asked them if they planned on approaching any girls that night. One of them responded, "I hear that when you go looking for a girl, you never find one. They say the best way to meet someone is to go out not expecting to meet anyone."

This is a popular misconception, one that has been fueled for years by people who have no idea of what they are talking about. The thinking here seems to be that the best way to meet someone is to do nothing at all. Believe me, this is the last thing a Shy Guy needs to hear. Shy Guys are experts at doing nothing. They work at it their whole lives. While it is true that sometimes girls do come your way when you're not expecting them to, the real truth is that those occasions are few and far between. If you sit around waiting for friends to hook you up, you may spend years alone, waiting for that hook-up to come.

The problem with this philosophy is that it implies that you have no control over your own destiny. This is nonsense. Each one of us has the ability to take charge of his own life. By sitting around and doing nothing, you are leaving everything to fate. You are essentially saying that the one thing in life that is most important to you is the one thing you have absolutely no control over.

This is a rather defeatist way to live, I think. If a girl is what you are looking for, then, by God, go out and look for her! It's easy to sit at home drowning in self-pity. The hard thing is to get up off your butt and actually do something to improve your life. Do you want to be passive forever?

When I was younger, my friend Bill used to have different theories about the type of guys who "always get girls." According to Bill, high school jocks always get girls. Dangerous-looking bikers always get girls. Long-haired rock 'n' rollers always get girls. Preppie college boys always get girls.

Basically, Bill was trying to rationalize the fact that he, me, and all our friends never got any girls. Heck, we didn't even *know* any girls! Apparently, it was because we didn't ride Harleys or wear sweaters tied around our necks or play guitars. But there was one important fact Bill was overlooking. There is one type of guy that always gets girls: Guys who try. That's all there is to it. If you try, you face the possibility of meeting girls. If you attempt nothing, more often than not, you get nothing.

So my advice to you is to try. I don't expect you to run up to the first girl you see and ask her out. You've got to start slowly. In the beginning, you'll have a lot of false starts before you learn how to close a deal. You may choose to bypass the singles bar route and go for the more comfortable methods of meeting girls, such as the Internet, singles dances, or personal ads.

You may decide to take a good look around the gym, the office, or the classroom, and find romance in those environments. You may take a closer look at your female friends, and decide to make a play for one of them. Whichever methods you choose, if there is a girl you are attracted to, then by all means, let her know.

Whether you get rejected or not, you'll be glad you tried. The rejections will hurt at first, but in time, you won't even feel them. Gradually your skin will get thickened to the point where you don't even notice them anymore.

Fear of rejection is the one thing that held me back the most in my early days. Rejection was this great, mysterious creature that could hurt me like no other. If ever I had to face this unconquerable beast, surely I would die. But face it I did. And while you can never completely kill this beast, at least I was able to drive it back into its cave, where it only occasionally rears its ugly head.

The important thing to remember is that you've got to try. If you don't try, you get nothing. If you try, you face the risk of rejection. But you also face the possibility of meeting a nice girl, and that's worth the risk. So what if she rejects you? Who cares? Just pick yourself up and move on to the next girl!

You're not going to let a little thing like fear of rejection hold you back now, are you?

Well, that's about it. I've said all I have to say. There's nothing more I can teach you. I like to think I've provided all of you with the role model I never had when I was a kid. In a sense, I've served as the Fonzie to your Richie. The Mr. Miyagi to your Karate Kid. The Kotter to your Horshack!

But ultimately, there's only so much even the Fonz could teach before he had to ride off on his bike and leave Richie to deal with his problems like a man. So from here on out, you're on your own. Don't worry, though. I think you'll do just fine. I've taught you the methods that have been time-tested by Shy Guys for generations. Follow some of my suggestions, and in no time at all, you'll go from Shy Guy to Aggressive Guy!

There may even be a girl looking at you right now, watching you read this book. Take a look at her. Try to catch her eye. Is she making eye contact? Say, she just might be! Why not go over to her and start up a conversation? Go ahead, she won't bite. The worst thing that can happen is she can say no.

You might as well walk over to her and tell her how nice she looks today. Go ahead, talk to her. She's waiting for you.

Don't be shy!